FIND,
FIX,
FILL
your
LEADERSHIP

GAP

what you need to know,
and no one is telling you

CANDICE GOTTLIEB-CLARK

FIND,
FIX,
FILL

your

LEADERSHIP

GAP

what you need to know,
and no one is telling you

CANDICE GOTTLIEB-CLARK

Paperback ISBN: 979-8-9856009-0-2

DTS
PUBLISHING

For every leader who cares about the people on their team and wants to help them thrive.

TABLE OF CONTENTS

PART THREE: FIX

PART FOUR: FILL

SPECIAL INVITATION

This book has been a labor of love. While I have several other books already on the horizon (including ones on teamwork and emotional intelligence), this is the first and most important. It is the launchpad for the others. Self-aware leaders are the key to healthy teams and successful businesses.

As a leader, you have your struggles. You have your own story to tell and lessons to learn. For that reason, I am currently developing a workshop around this book to offer more direct guidance to leaders who want to be the best that they can be—who know they have gaps and who are looking for direct support in finding, fixing, and filling those gaps. In tandem with the workshop, I am creating a self-study guide. Both provide you with opportunities for deeper learning and self-exploration. They are a part of the FIND FIX FILL Future.

I'd like to personally invite you to stay in touch and continue with me on this journey of developing leaders. You can connect with me at CandiceGottliebClark.com/grow, Facebook.com/groups/FindFixFill, or LinkedIn.com/in/CandiceGottliebClark.

Thank you so much for your time and commitment to becoming a self-aware leader. I am thrilled to be a part of your journey and your success.

INTRODUCTION

When I began my career as a workplace relations specialist, I had a simple and audacious goal to change the world of work. To create a world in which coming to work was a positive experience.

As the product of divorce, I grew up in a single-parent household. My mother was the financial and emotional supporter of our family. While she was a dutiful employee and cared about her job, she worked for a man who was demanding and at times verbally abusive. She stayed at that job out of necessity, but she was miserable, and her anger and frustration spilled out into our family on a near-daily basis. My mother's unhappiness and perhaps her sense of helplessness stayed with me and ignited my passion for creating change in the workplace.

More than a decade later, after completing my master's degree in counseling and working in several public, private, and government institutions, I stumbled upon the field of mediation and was immediately enamored by it. I dove in headfirst, learning all that I could. I accepted two job opportunities that afforded me a way to practice and develop my mediation skills almost daily. Soon after, I began to envision a way to use those skills to make the change I wanted to see in the world—where I could help those in a workplace setting communicate better, voice and resolve their conflict thoroughly, and find positive and collaborative ways of working together. I began Dynamic Team Solutions, then known as Mediating Solutions, to answer my calling.

During my first years as a consultant, I was steadfast and laser-focused on addressing issues of conflict. When a client hired me, I began the engagement by meeting with the business owner or leader who would connect me to the individuals or team in turmoil. They would pass the baton, then get back to their work. I had access and independence. My role was to work directly with the individuals experiencing conflict—to help them uncover and resolve the issues undermining their ability to work well together. My goal was to create a more collaborative and cohesive work environment.

The mediation process allowed me to help the individuals in conflict. The participants reached new levels of awareness, built understanding, identified ways to work successfully, and moved forward together. The process also illuminated problems that were likely to interfere with long-term change. I became aware of the impact the conflict had on others in the organization, and more importantly, the influencing factors that were underlying the conflict. Those elements are routinely connected with company leadership. I often found a manager or leader's behavior was linked to the conflict I had been called in to resolve.

It was clear to me their involvement had not been intentional, but that did nothing to lessen the impact of their actions. Nor was there any hope for improvement if those leaders were not aware of their relationship to the issue. The problems would resurface, wreaking havoc with new people.

That posed an unexpected challenge. I had to ensure that the pertinent feedback reached the leader.

Not surprisingly, the employees I'd helped—even when they could identify the leader's role—were not given to engaging with their leader about it. The potential for career suicide was not very appealing. That meant it would have to be me. I would have to tell the person who had hired me that they were a fundamental part of the problem.

That created an obvious predicament. Not only would delivering the information be desperately uncomfortable, but it would also make me and my business vulnerable to several potential consequences. I could lose future business with the client, jeopardize the likelihood the client would refer me to others, receive negative feedback on social media or in professional settings, etc. I might also find the client reluctant to pay the balance of my fees.

Nevertheless, I understood that to create a positive work environment, I had no option but to inform the leaders of the unpleasant truth.

I quickly found this situation proved to be the rule, not the exception. After having survived a few very uncomfortable conversations, I realized I would need a strategy for making this conversation a lot less stressful.

I began engaging with my clients differently. Before taking on a project, during our "getting to know you" phase, I began to simply ask the leader, "If I find that some of the issues lead back to you, how do you want me to let you know?" Not only did that simple and direct question save the leader and me a lot of discomfort, it also built a readiness for me to hold those difficult conversations when the time came.

I was pleasantly surprised by the responses I received. Every leader I asked gave a willing and open response to my question. Many openly stated that they were sure they *did* have a connection to the issues. Approaching those leaders with the details of their culpability was still uncomfortable, but it was tremendously helpful. It laid the groundwork for sharing.

That was the first kernel of knowledge telling me I should write this book. Leaders wanted to know how they could lead and manage their teams better. They were open to hearing the information and to creating change. They were simply lacking in the information they needed. They were experiencing a feedback gap.

THE CONCEPT OF FIND, FIX, FILL YOUR LEADERSHIP GAP WAS BORN.

What you are about to read is not a research book filled with references to studies and authors. It is not a collection of the work of others, repackaged for your consumption. Rather this book is a reflection of my experiences in working with over 500 leaders and executives who needed support to address the chaos occurring in their work environments. It is a glimpse into their world, and perhaps yours, through the lens of a workplace and interpersonal relations specialist.

True, much of what I will teach connects to the work of giants in the fields of social and work dynamics. You will see references to Brené Brown, Adam Grant, Simon Sinek, James Clear, and others. Where *FIND, FIX,*

FILL is different is that it is based on real-world leaders who, while doing their very best, still made choices that created conflict, silos, loss of talent, and more.

As I teach you about the leadership gap, I will illuminate the common issues leaders face (FIND) and share strategies to shore up those gaps (FIX). I'll do this through several true stories. After those problems have been identified and resolved, I'll help build your arsenal of skills (FILL) to help you become the best leader you can be.

My hope is that these stories and lessons allow you to FIND, FIX, and FILL your own leadership gap. Once you have, you will be able to develop and lead a powerful, focused, engaged, and collaborative team—a team where the individuals don't simply want to come to work but who actively want to work *with* each other.

Through my stories, you'll see leaders who have been where you are or where you could soon be. The stories offer context and expose complicated circumstances; they paint the picture of the problems (such as poor accountability and teamwork issues) caused by leaders and explain why. They will help you to see how easy it is for a leader (perhaps even you) to make the wrong choice yet never be able to see it.

As a professional speaker, I often share these and other stories to illustrate a lesson, and the stories always resonate. Time and again, audience members come forward to share how familiar the stories are to them—how they identify with the characters or the lesson. Some have suggested it's as if I've been inside their company walls watching them or their leadership.

I believe these stories resonate because they are a product of our humanity and the universality of working relationships. They reveal our desires to do well, be liked, and please others, alongside the challenges we each face in seeing our own foibles.

Over the past twenty years, I have had the privilege of working with hundreds of companies and thousands of employees. I have spent countless hours interviewing individuals who are involved in conflict or are experiencing interpersonal tensions that impact their work. I have been privy to the challenging workplace circumstances these individuals face while maintaining objectivity as a workplace relations consultant. That has allowed me to see and understand the causes of those tensions, for trends to become evident, and patterns of behavior clear.

As I share this hard-fought knowledge with you, you may see yourself in my stories. You may recognize similar qualities in your leadership. Great! You're in the right place. Mistakes are essential to growth. Rather than criticizing, shaming, or condemning, I will focus on building your awareness, developing your learning, and helping you create new strategies for change.

I've often been called an eternal optimist. I look for (and find) the bright side in every situation. While I consider myself to be realistic, I prefer to see opportunities, not limitations.

This continues even when I work with difficult people. I believe the best in them. Rather than accept that they are bad people, I work to understand what drives their behavior.

I COINED A PHILOSOPHY BASED ON THIS: VINDICATE; DON'T VILLAINIZE.

Even when working with someone who exhibits egregious behavior, I maintain a perspective that they have reasons I don't yet understand. I look to find *their* rationale—to gain an understanding of the drivers beneath their behavior. Being open-minded and seeking to find the good in others has allowed me to build trust with these "difficult" people. Trust is the starting point, allowing me to bring about change.

Throughout this book, I'll remind you: vindicate; don't villainize—to adjust your perspective so that you can see what lies beneath the surface.

WHAT I WANT FOR YOU

FIND. FIX. FILL Your Leadership Gap was written to help you become the leader you want to be—to allow you to create a positive work environment for yourself, your teams, and your company.

As you read, I will be taking you on a journey . . . or three. I will bring you along to explore the situations of three different clients I have served. I will share the problems, their causes, and lessons learned. While some of the clients in the book know that they have been included, others do not. Regardless, to protect the privacy of all, I have changed the names and certain characteristics of the organizations to provide anonymity for the individuals and businesses described. While I have strived for accuracy in telling these stories, the passage of time has likely affected my memory of some of the specifics. But that in no way affects the stories or their lessons.

In Part 1 — The GAP — I expose why a leadership gap exists, how it grows, and how it leads to an ever-expanding abyss of information. You don't know what you don't know. Part 1 will help you recognize not only what causes the gap but how the gap impacts your success as a leader.

In Part 2 — FIND — I share three distinct leadership stories. I include the circumstances, situations, and aftermath. I bring to light the gap between what the leader intended and the actual outcomes of their actions. In some cases, I share my professional insights about what drove the behavior or about the individual fears or concerns governing the actions of those involved. You will get a glimpse into what I see and learn, what is revealed, and what is not. That is what I experience when working intimately with my clients on conflict issues.

In FIND, I will introduce you to the three attributes essential for healthy leadership: trust, role clarity, and conflict management. I will help you see how these attributes influence and inform a leader's success.

In Part 3 — FIX — I dissect each of the stories you read in FIND. I expand on each story, identifying the lessons that can be learned from them. This section provides detailed guidance on what to do and *not* do as you strive to FIX your leadership gap.

In FIX, I connect the attributes of trust, role clarity, and conflict management to the issues each leader faced, allowing you to bridge the learning with *your* leadership style. As you go through Part 3, you will begin to see how to FIX your leadership gap.

FIX is devoted to identifying the "What" and providing the "How." What did the leader need to know? What did the leader need to change? How did the leader incorporate those lessons to bring about change? How did their efforts make a difference? FIX will teach you what you need to change, allowing you to quickly improve the dynamics of your team and in your organization.

In Part 4 — FILL — I continue to fill your strategy bucket. Beyond the lessons you can learn from each story, I share insights that will help you grow as a leader. FILL will broaden your perspective for building trust and managing conflict. You will find your point of view continues to shift as I expose how the traditional paradigm of leadership has distorted the reality of your role.

FILL allows me to teach you where, when, and why to adjust or engage in different strategies to support your team and enhance your leadership. Beyond new insights, you will learn how to hit the Refresh button and reengage your team when things have gotten off track.

FILL continues to build your skills and competency as a leader so that you can create a strong, cohesive, and resilient team—a team that displays strong trust and great accountability and can support one another and catapult the business forward.

Finally, Part 5 — Other Lessons. Here, I attend to all the connecting points that didn't fit nicely into FILL. In "Other Lessons," I provide detailed step-by-step instructions for engaging in a difficult or critical conversation, allowing you to confidently engage with your team, peers, or leaders about challenging situations. In this section, I also expose how individual accountability is directly impacted by the attributes of trust, role clarity, and conflict management and how you can adjust the influence and, therefore, the accountability you see on your team.

I wrap up Part 5 by revisiting our three leaders, with the chapter, "Where are they now?" This closing section will not only provide you with closure on each story but will also act as a cautionary tale of what can happen when you do not FIND. FIX. FILL Your Leadership Gap.

Before you read on, I'd like to share an absolute truth about leadership. Having good intentions is never enough. If it were, you wouldn't be reading this, and I wouldn't have written it. This is not a book about intention; it is a book about reality. It is a book that offers lessons you cannot get elsewhere.

Whether you are a first-time manager, a seasoned director, a member of the executive team, or the owner of the business, this book is for you. Your readiness to examine your leadership and your willingness to grow and change will define your success and the success of those who report to you.

Your skills and awareness define your way of interacting with others. Your leadership determines the strength, capacity, and cohesion of your teams. You make a profound difference in the success of others and impact the survival of your organization. This book will build the awareness you need to lead with success.

You are probably familiar with the expression . . .

There are things that I know.

There are things that I know I do not know.

And finally,

There are the things that I do not know I do not know.

The first two statements reflect the information we can identify for ourselves. We can teach or share what we know. We can ask for help or seek to learn things that we do not know. These are areas of our awareness. It is that final statement, the *things I do not know I do not know* that leaves us in an abyss.

FIND. FIX. FILL Your Leadership Gap was written to help you see through the abyss of leadership and human relations. It sheds light on things you don't know but need to know to be an exceptional and self-aware leader. Let's get started. It's time to FIND, FIX, and FILL Your Leadership Gap.

PART ONE

THE GAP

CHAPTER ONE

UNDERSTANDING THE GAP

None of us is an expert in leadership.
The practice of leadership is a journey, and we are all students.

—Simon Sinek

In my work with organizations, I have found one of the underlying challenges affecting all leaders is the feedback gap—the gap between what the leader knows and what she does not know. There is always a gap between what others share and what they withhold. It is in this space that information is lacking, and feedback is needed.

A gap exists for every leader—from the confident and self-assured leader to the leader who employs false bravado to convince others of his ability. Even humble and servant leaders, eager to support others and receive reciprocal feedback, experience a feedback gap as they, based on title or stature, are held up on a pedestal by those around them.

The truth is, we all rely on others to inform and guide us—to share their wisdom and offer their advice, but once you've become a leader, that essential guidance stops.

SOURCES OF THE GAP

Presumptions

Part of the feedback gap comes from the presumption that you, as the leader, know more than everyone reporting to you. The anticipated knowledge may come from your education and credentials, past work experiences, or simply your access to information. People unquestioningly trust in your commensurate ability and knowledge based solely on your title and background. They will hold fast to the idea that you know what you are doing or, at the very least, know more than they do.

Even among those who realize you don't know *everything*, there exists a resistance to pointing out the problems, correcting you, or offering enlightenment. The reluctance to share connects to fears of repercussion, the desire to save face, and our need for self-preservation.

Even those who *want* to provide help must carefully weigh the circumstances and potential consequences. Are they sure they are right? How can they be? Is it worth the risk? The inevitable reluctance to inform you creates a syndrome like the emperor's new clothes. Even when the whole kingdom sees you in all your naked splendor, only the fool or most naïve will inform you of those facts.

Likability

A well-liked leader will fall victim to the feedback gap just as quickly as the one without team support. Leaders with supportive teams are equally susceptible to a vacuum of information. I've seen this play out many times. The more your staff likes you, the *less* they want to point out your flaws. Instead, they find ways to work around your inadequacies, sometimes actively shielding you from feedback. They may do so to save your ego, but more often, their efforts are self-serving, intended to secure your position as their leader. They like you and want to continue to work with you.

The leader who is not well-liked will receive limited feedback for different reasons. These leaders lack a legitimate bond with their team. They are typically lacking in basic interpersonal and communication skills. Who is going to help someone they don't like? Who is going to be vulnerable in presenting feedback to someone they don't trust? The only feedback these leaders will receive will come by way of an ambush, with the information being used to damage their career or undermine their success.

Self-Imposed Gaps

Leaders cause their own gaps as well. I have no doubt that there are things you are unsure of. Things you know you do not know. But whom do you tell? Do you share that secret with anyone? Your spouse? Best friend? Mentor? Most likely, you share your concerns with no one. Instead, you go it alone. You read books, listen to podcasts, and hope to make the right choices. But none completely fills your void. The gap persists.

Mentors and Peers

Peers and mentors are not reliable sources of feedback either. They are uncomfortable sharing their observations, do not feel they have the authority or responsibility to intervene, or do not want to hear reciprocal feedback about themselves. Some possess professional aspirations that limit their willingness to help you. They withhold feedback if they see you as competition or believe your weaknesses will help secure their own power or position.

The Top Brass

A leader's final hope for feedback may come from those who monitor their success. But this, too, falls short. Unlike an employee with several peers and a manager or supervisor overseeing their work and professional interactions, a leader is often alone to evaluate their own performance. There is a profound absence of oversight and no one to illuminate the blind spots. A Board of Directors, while often holding this responsibility, cannot provide anywhere close to the same guidance or feedback for an executive director or CEO as a manager would to their direct report. Not only does a board member rarely have the time or inclination to do so, but they also lack sufficient perspective to identify a problem. More to the point, a board is not typically interested in this level of oversight unless they are looking to remove the leader from the organization.

That points to the final barrier. Any leader with a survival instinct is motivated to cloud (hide) any gap of knowledge they possess from the board or other top brass overseeing their performance.

A Reluctance to Ask

Despite the prevalence of these gaps, few leaders take the necessary steps to close those gaps.

Leaders, while fully capable of asking for feedback from their teams, rarely do. Many wouldn't know what to ask or where they lack skill; it is part of the abyss. And let's face it: asking is not comfortable. It creates a perception of weakness. It suggests that others have more knowledge or could be more capable. Leaders don't ask for help because asking calls into question their ability to fulfill their role.

Every aspect of missed feedback creates a blind spot—a large, gaping hole in what a leader needs to know. This is not a motivation gap. In my experience, most leaders are motivated to improve. They just prefer to do it on their own terms. Books, podcasts, and other areas of self-improvement support this.

How, then, does a leader who is shrouded by gaps of knowledge and a lack of feedback become aware of what they need to know or how they need to change?

FIND. FIX. FILL.

Because we have blind spots, we need to engage others as a part of our ability to see. We need to invite others to share, provide feedback, and help us to become more aware. We need them to shine a light on that abyss.

This book will address the abyss. The chasm that occurs—and grows—out of the feedback gap, which all leaders have.

Our client, Episcopal Communities and Services (ECS), engaged with us to address their leadership gap. Their goal was to ensure their leaders could find their areas of weakness and opportunities for improvement.

A nonprofit organization that supports senior living communities, ECS emphasizes supporting their employees just as ardently as they do their residents. They believe in personal and professional development. At ECS, social accountability is the essence that underlies its core values.

Those robust and self-affirming efforts helped create a culture within ECS that is dedicated and caring. Leaders recognize that feedback is connected to opportunity, so they routinely provide support, guidance, and feedback to their staff.

However, despite that dedication, the executive leaders were at a loss. Who could provide them with these opportunities? How could they grow and develop? How can they be the leaders their team members need if they lack insight into their own areas for growth? Who would be willing to share that information candidly enough for it to be of value?

The leaders at ECS saw the abyss. As described by their Vice President of Human Resources . . .

"As we were rewriting our business plan and vision for the next ten years or so, we concluded that we needed to make sure that our senior leadership team was a cohesive group and that we were all driving in the same direction.

"We like to think that we're all completely honest with each other and in our meetings, but people are not naïve. There's always a limit to what we're willing to say and do . . . so that it's not a detriment to ourselves. We know that when there's a reporting relationship, we're not going to get good data.

"That's why we chose to engage Dynamic Team Solutions in conducting a 360 evaluation for our team. It created a space where our team could talk to someone independently. A consultant met with each of us and asked the questions we hadn't thought of. Through that effort, we got feedback that we believe will be useful to each leader.

"We decided to take that initial feedback and use it as a baseline. It was not connected with a performance evaluation but instead was the opportunity for each of us to see how other people were seeing us. To identify the strengths and opportunities for making a change. We then explored our results as a whole *team to see where our gaps are and how we could work better together."*

—Stacie Ocampo, VP of Human Resources,
Episcopal Communities and Services

The leaders of ECS were replete with self-awareness. They recognized that they could not possibly identify what to change or why by simply approaching those on their team and asking.

It was clear that ECS was aware of the gap and ready to close it. But they were far from alone in this effort.

In all my work with businesses, I have never encountered a leader who didn't care about their team. Nor have I ever worked with one who intentionally created or allowed problems to occur. In many cases, it was the leader who sought my services or brought me in. Nevertheless, many leaders I have met—particularly those included in this book—made choices that created problems. But they did not do so with malicious intent. On the contrary, they did their best given the tools and knowledge available to them. Sadly, though, that is often not enough.

The leadership missteps discussed in this book are not intended to villainize any of these leaders but rather to vindicate them, to show how most leaders—indeed most people—might easily have made the same choices and taken the same steps.

Shame has no place here. Mistakes are not our focus. Instead, they are tools useful for illuminating opportunities for growth.

Accepting that you have a feedback gap, a blind spot, an abyss of knowledge is the first step toward fixing and filling that gap. The good news is you're not in this alone.

CHAPTER TWO

PATTERNS AND PREDICTABILITY

Marsha comes into the office at 8:15 a.m. She walks into her office, sets down her things, starts her computer, and leaves to get her first cup of coffee.

She passes Tyler on her way and gives him a cursory nod.

She returns a few minutes later and sits down at her desk to begin the day.

Tyler needs to speak with Marsha. There is a complication with the project he is running, and he needs her input. But Tyler waits.

Marsha is rarely in the office this early. She didn't engage with him beyond acknowledging his presence.

He presumes she has an early meeting to prepare for. He will need her to be focused when they speak. He decides the conversation can wait until that afternoon.

As the afternoon approaches, Marsha seems even less accessible. Tyler, aware that he cannot delay the conversation further, begs for a moment of her time.

Marsha, however, is fully engulfed in addressing another situation. She is distracted as she listens to Tyler's issue, then angered when she learns that it was identified the day prior. The ensuing conversation between the two is stilted, fueled by frustration and a lack of time.

The input Tyler receives is superficial, and the exchange leaves both Tyler and Marsha unsatisfied and disappointed. The experience colors the profile each has created of the other.

We are all geared to notice patterns. Marsha's early arrival signaled to Tyler that there was a critical reason for it. He respected her reasons without knowing them. The pattern he saw was interpreted as: early arrival = work to do! However, Marsha's early arrival was not a deliberate effort to address a specific need. Instead, it was to get a jump on things—a commitment to stay ahead of the crises that always seemed to erupt in the mid-afternoon. Tyler's delay in sharing details of the problem before him meant she had an uneventful morning but an impossible afternoon—just what she had sought to avoid.

While Marsha and Tyler are fictional, their situation is not. Imagine for a moment the views each might now hold of the other.

Tyler's view: Marsha is impatient. Unconcerned. She doesn't recognize the gravity of the situation I've uncovered. She has no business being a manager or leader.

Tyler's view may extend to a rationalization that Marsha is trying to set him up for failure by offering limited help and guidance.

Marsha's view: Tyler is a slacker. He was in early when it was quiet and she was available, but he chose to wait until there was complete chaos in the office before bringing an important issue to me. She wonders, *Is he a bumbling fool, or is he trying to undermine me?*

Marsha becomes less trusting of Tyler and increases her oversight of his activities.

Marsha and Tyler illustrate the underpinnings of the struggle between leaders and their team members. There are patterns that exist. Patterns in the way a leader responds, communicates, and behaves toward her team. Patterns in the reaction or response she receives from her staff. Patterns equate to predictability. Tyler predicted, based on Marsha's early arrival and cursory greeting, that she had an important meeting to prepare for.

Being predictable can support fluidity among the team. Had Marsha needed the morning to prepare, this would have been helpful. Predictability allows each person to know what is expected and how to perform. But it can lead to making the wrong assumptions. Patterns are not exact.

A secondary point for consideration is that predictability is not necessarily positive or constructive. A leader is just as given to developing patterns that create conflict, undermine teamwork, or interfere with productivity. Tyler may now recognize Marsha as resentful when he brings up an issue. Marsha may believe Tyler is attempting to sabotage her role as the leader.

We notice patterns in others, detecting commonalities in behaviors or responses. This allows us to make decisions and learn what to expect from others. But we don't all see patterns the same way. And most certainly, we do not readily see our own patterns.

Each decision you make, each action you take comes from reasons known only to you. The nuances of experience and thought impacting your decision-making are like an elaborate mosaic. For that reason, identifying your patterns is never easy.

While the experiences that validate your behaviors and actions are unique, they are still seen as patterns by others. In much the same way, I see past the idiosyncratic qualities of each leader and notice the common patterns—those which underlie their struggle and that of their teams.

My perspective is not jaded by past interactions, deep knowledge of the individuals involved, or concerns about the company's clients or deliverables. I'm focused on the people, the problems, and the patterns.

While I am always happy to work with businesses like ECS, whose goals are proactive, I have spent the bulk of my career helping those in the throes of chaos. Or, at the very least, who recognize that they are operating with a level of dysfunction that is not acceptable to them.

The issues they are facing often include concerns about team conflict, loss of talent, problems with accountability, and experiencing a persistent or growing number of complaints. Sometimes HR or company leaders recognize a pattern has developed or pinpoint a leader or team member who is commonly associated with the turmoil. Most have attempted to resolve these issues internally but to no avail.

These companies invite me into their vault. They share the depth of their struggles with me. They grant me access to people and information. They allow me to ask questions and probe for details. Far from being closed, they hope I will find the source of the problems they are experiencing so that I may improve their situation. It is an honor to be trusted in that role.

The initial part of my process includes interviewing employees. I ask questions to learn about current issues and historical situations. I hear about the people they like to work with as well as those whom they avoid or struggle to engage with. I learn about the ways the team interacts and how the leader behaves. In short, I am given access to the emotional experience of working together.

Through the kaleidoscope of information I receive, I have come to recognize the fundamental struggles common among all leaders. These are consistent and familiar struggles, all arising from the same core issues: trust, role clarity, and conflict management.

The stories, comments, and situations I hear from both the leader and others always filter back to these core issues.

Note: The questions below are *not* ones I directly ask. Instead, they are the byproduct and reflections I have based on the answers I receive.

Trust – Does the leader trust his team? Does the team trust its leader? Do the team members operate with trust in one another? Does the leader find himself in the middle, managing tension between others?

Role Clarity – Is the leader fulfilling her job, her role? Is she holding her team accountable for their roles? Does each person know what is expected of them? Does each understand what they are (and are not) responsible for? Do they know how their work interconnects with that of others in the organization?

Conflict Management – Does the leader actively attend to issues that create conflict, or does he sweep issues under the rug? Does he look for root causes or engage in quick fixes? Does the leader, through action or inaction, *create* situations of conflict?

Like a three-legged stool, each of these three attributes—trust, role clarity, and conflict management—affects the other two. None occurs in isolation. Each lays an impact on the struggles of a team.

Ironically, complaints of the leader—about their team's commitment, accountability, work ethic, or drive—directly relate to these core issues. The struggle of the leader becomes the struggle for the team. Trust, role clarity and conflict management are fundamental to the workplace experience. Understanding and altering your relationship with each of these qualities is the key to creating lasting change.

Sections FIND, FIX, FILL will expose each of these three struggles and provide guidance for strengthening each leg of the stool. As we move into Part 2 — FIND — the revelations will begin. I will share stories of three different leaders and their teams. I will expose the situations that led each to seek help, as well as the circumstances I encountered while working with the leader and individual members of the team. As we move through each story, you will better understand the impact and cross-related nature of the core issues I've described. You may see parallels to your situation or notice your own struggles in their stories. FIND is where we begin to identify the issues affecting your role as a leader.

PART TWO

FIND

INTRODUCTION TO FIND

The great leaders are not the strongest;
they are the ones who are honest about their weaknesses.

The great leaders are not the smartest;
they are the ones who admit how much they don't know.

The great leaders can't do everything;
they are the ones who look to others to help them.

Great leaders don't see themselves as great;
they see themselves as human.

—Simon Sinek

Executives rise to their position of leadership from many different backgrounds—through the ranks, brought in from outside, starting their own company, and more. Each arrives with his unique strengths and weaknesses, skills, and behaviors. These govern his actions, decisions, and leadership abilities. Similarly, they lead to his blind spots, feedback gaps, and related challenges.

This section—FIND—will take you to the beginning by telling the story of three different leaders. Except for crediting direct quotes, all names in this book have been changed to protect individual identities.

Stuart – the up-and-comer. Ready to take on his new role with enthusiasm and lead with integrity.

Gary – the reformer. Brought on to create change within a large educational institution.

Josephine – the legacy. Deeply committed to the organization's success.

All three are caring, dedicated, and hardworking. Yet each of these leaders experienced the feedback gap, and though they were doing their best, they still fell victim to not knowing what they did not know.

By hearing the stories and situations of Stuart, Gary, and Josephine, you will come to recognize how each of these leaders comes by their gaps honestly. Within Part 2 — FIND — I will use their experiences as a teaching point, identifying the lessons each leader's foibles provide.

You will understand why seemingly positive actions and decisions can result in dramatic tensions and painful problems. FIND is your place for vicarious learning. From the safety of your reading (or listening) spot, you will learn how a leader acting with good intention can undermine his and his team's success.

As you read their stories, I have no doubt there will be familiarity. You may get a glimpse into situations similar to your own or to those you've witnessed in others. You will begin to see the intersection of trust, role clarity, and conflict management. FIND is the beginning. It provides you with the wisdom and heightened awareness to FIND your patterns, change, and grow.

CHAPTER THREE

STUART

Stuart felt charged and ready when the prominent labor union he had been leading for two years voted to expand its structures for employee representation. He had been lobbying for this change from the start. He was responsible for overseeing all elements of the union's activities to date. While he was able to develop plans and guide progress in supporting the board's overarching vision, he was limited in his ability to bring about meaningful change. This was Stuart's first role as executive director. At last, with another tier of leadership, it would now be possible. The board understood that oversight and direct support would be integral to the success of the expansion.

Stuart was charged with building the team of directors who would report to him. Those directors, in turn, would manage the large staff of employees Stuart had been overseeing. Stuart felt excited and very much up for the challenge. He would find the dedicated professionals needed to drive the union's initiatives forward. And, with their added support, he could focus his energy on the big picture.

Stuart was deeply motivated to create an outstanding team. He knew the stakes were high and that there would be challenges in developing a new tier within the organization. He knew that his ability to do this well would define not only *his* success but that of the union itself. Just hitting the prime of his career, Stuart was full of energy and ideas. After examining the initiatives and goals, Stuart identified the positions he would need to create and fill on this team.

Beginning in the recruitment phase, Stuart engaged with each potential team member, getting to know them, their drive, and their commitment. He was determined to hire only bright, capable, and motivated people.

Once he hired his dream team, he spent more time getting to know each one, building the foundation of their relationship. The more time he spent, the more convinced he became of each person's commitment and capability to support the organization's goals. He was building trust as he built the team.

Stuart was gifted in identifying talent and building interest and engagement in the organizational goals. He did hire exceptionally well. But despite having brought on talented and motivated individuals, it became apparent within the first year that all was not well with the team.

Though highly competent and skillful, this group of directors who reported to Stuart had begun forming significant complaints about one another. More to the point, beyond the more commonplace individual complaints, nearly the whole team had joined forces in protest about one member of the group: Oliver.

Oliver, whose role largely kept him outside of the organization's walls, was the recipient of the team's animosity. The team didn't find him to be a team player. He shrugged off accountability, and he wasn't around enough to build trust with his fellow directors.

Oliver had also built a reputation with the team for overreaching and stepping on their toes. The team had seen a concerning pattern emerge of Oliver engaging in discussions outside his purview. While meeting with company stakeholders, he would delve into marketing ideas and thoughts for advancing organizational initiatives. While it was not his area of expertise, Oliver was cavalier about his behavior, taking on this role even as his team complained. As Oliver saw it, there was nothing wrong with floating his ideas to influential affiliates outside the organization. He had meetings with them anyway. If an idea came to him during their meeting, why not run it by them? If the idea took root, he would surely inform the rest of the team.

However, Oliver's actions and subsequent commitments had a direct impact on several members of the team, none more so than Kate, the director of marketing. Oliver's actions directly undermined and dismissed her knowledge and authority.

Kate was responsible for the organization's initiatives and ensuring all marketing efforts were well-targeted. She held the ultimate authority for determining the marketing plan and its associated budget.

Oliver's inexpert ideas, once "sold" to stakeholders, complicated matters. His meddling set in motion a program rife with flaws that would need to be overcome.

Kate and her team felt the impact and the fury. Their activities and focus were entirely altered by Oliver's actions. They could no longer plan ahead with the most effective strategy. Her team's role became one of reactive cleanup rather than proactive planning.

While he held no role or authority greater than any of the other directors, Oliver's overstepping pattern reached almost every internal group member.

Frustrated by his behavior, several directors brought their concerns to Oliver. They saw little in the way of results.

Oliver didn't see himself as accountable to the team. He typically bowed out of team meetings. He didn't respond to their phone calls, and his voice mail was often full.

When Kate or one of the other team members approached Oliver directly to discuss their concerns, he would seem agreeable and set up a time but would then skip the appointment. An effort to reach out to him would be met with an emailed response citing that he was needed in the field.

Unable to bring about change, the affected directors began to complain to one another, venting and sharing their feelings of exasperation.

As frustrations mounted and things escalated, the directors sought their leader's support. Stuart listened to his team and committed to speaking with Oliver about the issues.

Understandably, the team expected results. Stuart was the leader. Oliver would have to listen to him. The group envisioned Oliver now attending directors' meetings, responding to their calls and emails, and communicating more openly about organizational matters. But nothing notable changed. More to the point, new issues continued to arise.

In the weeks that followed, Oliver failed to roll up his sleeves to support a costly initiative he instigated. When approached about the need for his involvement, Oliver demurred. Then, aggravating the team further, he deflected responsibility for the problems which arose from the ill-conceived plan.

As the team saw it, Oliver created a problem, dumped it on them, and then deserted them. The team was up in arms.

The team felt certain Stuart was ready to take Oliver to task.

But Stuart didn't seem concerned by this turn of events. If anything, he appeared to defend Oliver, explaining away Oliver's behavior, citing excuses similar to those Oliver had provided.

The team became incensed by Stuart's nonchalance. They pressed him for action. Feeling the team was out of line, Stuart denied further discussion on the topic.

Let's stop for a moment and unpack this.

Stuart, who had agreed to address a director's lack of accountability to the team, found that his efforts failed to bring desired results. It happens. Stuart cannot control Oliver. He can only address the issues, provide guidance, and engage in disciplinary action if necessary. Yet when Oliver neglected to change, Stuart did not respond to his team's concern that accountability was missing. Instead, he displayed support for the dysfunctional team member. Worse, he dismissed their concerns by shutting down further discussion. That moment shifted the anger and blame away from Oliver and onto Stuart.

The team quickly became convinced that Stuart had never spoken to Oliver or, at least, had not been clear about the need for Oliver to change. They guessed that Stuart hadn't taken their issues seriously or that possibly he was in over his head when it came to managing their colleague. Out of their growing dissatisfaction, the directors recognized change would need to come from them. They decided to take matters into their own hands. They planned to meet with Oliver en masse to get things straightened out. Surely Oliver couldn't deny or excuse an entire team sharing the same concerns.

The next time Oliver was in the office, the team seized their opportunity. They pulled Oliver into a closed-door meeting where they shared their frustrations over his failures to communicate, attend meetings, and pull his own weight. They gave specific examples of the challenges his actions had caused them. They described their having to "drop everything" at the last minute to attend to commitments *he* had made. They spoke of the costs to them personally, including the added stress of working late and missing time with their families. Finally, they pointed out the tangible costs he brought the organization in the form of paying employees overtime and managing the expense of last-minute, not to mention poorly thought-out marketing campaigns.

Oliver was caught entirely off guard. He hedged. He said what he needed to say in order to extricate himself from the meeting. Then, without acknowledging the problems he had caused the team, he approached Stuart and focused the conversation solely on his having been ambushed by the team.

Stuart listened. Then, wanting to regain control of the situation, he told Oliver that everything would be fine. He reassured Oliver that he'd speak with the rest of the team.

While Stuart typically focused on smoothing things over, he was furious with his team for confronting Oliver in the manner they had. He felt undermined. He saw it as a lack of respect that his team would go around him and "ambush" Oliver. He felt injured that the group had not trusted his leadership and capacity to manage the situation.

Stuart called together his team, sans Oliver, in an attempt to manage the conflict already present. Once gathered, he expressed his anger at their going around him and not trusting him. He reprimanded them for their actions. Then, he decided to level the playing field. Stuart began taking each member to task. He called out their flaws and mistakes. He pointed to Kate's having thrown up her arms in frustration over a project to another director who frequently lost his temper and to a third who had often scrambled to meet a deadline. As Stuart saw it, they had all acted inappropriately. They had all made mistakes.

Stuart's goal was to neutralize the energy directed at Oliver. But the impact of his pointing out each member's flaws brought only outrage. His attempts at conflict management undermined the team's trust in him and undercut his role as their leader.

The team was caught off guard by Stuart's accusations, but they pushed back. They agreed that everyone makes mistakes, but Oliver didn't acknowledge his mistakes. Nor did he accept responsibility for his impact on the team. Nor did he pitch in to help or show any other level of accountability to the team. And Stuart wasn't doing anything about it. Oliver was showing no willingness to change his behaviors. He would simply give lip service to get out of a discussion, then continue to engage in the same problem behaviors. Stuart needed to do something!

Stuart's effort to shift the directors' focus off Oliver and onto themselves was made with the hope of defusing the tension, but that was far from the result. Instead, the team shifted their focus onto him. Stuart's leadership was coming into question.

After the meeting, the team searched for answers in an effort to make sense of the situation. They concluded that Stuart was protecting Oliver. Naturally, they began to speculate why. Could Oliver have hidden information about Stuart? Was this favoritism? Questions continued to mount as the team assessed Stuart and Oliver's relationship. Their conversations took on a gossipy nature as the group began sharing their thoughts and rationales and ultimately fanning the flames of their own discord.

The more the group focused on Stuart's failure to fulfill his role in managing Oliver, the more they began to notice other flaws in his leadership: his inability to support them in front of the board and his reluctance to intervene when a committee member ignored protocol, became directive of their work, or was demanding of them. Whereas before, the team had commiserated *with* Stuart about overreach by the board or a committee member's antics, now they viewed it as Stuart's inability or unwillingness to create and support necessary boundaries. Things continued to deteriorate as the team lost trust in Stuart and began to distance themselves from him.

The team felt Stuart was an ineffective leader who was abdicating his responsibilities and leaving the team exposed.

Stuart, focused on his own experience, felt wronged and deserving of the team's trust and respect.

The chasm between them was becoming insurmountable. The elite and dedicated members of the group began expressing interest in leaving the organization.

FINDING THE GAP – THE LEADER'S ABYSS

The situation among this team may have seemed dire, but things weren't beyond repair. As the team already knew, the central figure needing to change was Stuart. While Oliver and the board had more directly brought about the team's frustrations and concerns, it was Stuart who needed to protect his team and ensure that problems were resolved.

Like many leaders, Stuart was out of his element when managing interpersonal issues. While he had been exceptional at building the team, managing that team was a skill set he had not mastered. His experience was limited to giving directives and strategic planning, not creating collaboration. He had limited experience in managing professionals he admired—particularly those with their own domain and level of authority.

The role of a leader, in its simplest form, must be to identify goals, set the direction of the team, and remove obstacles to success.

Stuart had mastered the first: identify goals. The team knew the organizational goals and purpose. They felt included and informed about what was due to be accomplished.

Stuart attempted the second: setting the direction of the team. But he had not been clear in delineating individual roles or boundaries. The team was left to determine that on their own.

Stuart seemed unaware of the third: removing obstacles to success. He mistakenly expected everyone to know their boundaries and stay in line with their own role without further clarification, support, or guidance.

It wasn't just the team's roles that needed further exploration. Stuart hadn't fully identified the gamut of his role as leader. He lacked clarity of how to simultaneously lead and manage his team. He struggled to organize them individually and as a collective. And he lacked an appreciation for the impact of his actions. Compounding the situation, Stuart wasn't prepared to manage workplace conflict.

While these issues were culminating in disaster for Stuart, they are not uncommon among leaders. All leaders make mistakes. Stuart is human. He's kind. He trusted his gut and acted on instinct. Like most leaders, he received only cursory training to help him develop the leadership skills he would need to excel. His repertoire was built largely on personal experience and the preferences he'd had when working under other leaders. As a result, Stuart's response to his team's actions—getting angry, spreading blame, and shutting down further communication about the issues—was not in line with his professional role. It was a gut reaction based on personal feelings. When his team lost trust in him, Stuart felt betrayed.

Stuart's leadership abyss included these issues :

- Trust
- Role Clarity
- Conflict Management

TRUST

Stuart misunderstood the leader's role in developing trust. Instead of focusing on creating fluidity, collaboration, and shared organizational goals, Stuart placed his energy on developing a warm relationship with each team member. He sought to build trust in the way most comfortable for him—out of friendship. It began during his recruitment of the team and continued to grow from there.

Stuart was proud to know each member of his team as a person, not an employee. He knew about their lives, and he cared about them. He believed it would be vital to a healthy, trusting, and successful relationship with his team. However, Stuart missed the boat by focusing so intently on individual trust. He overlooked the significance of having the team members develop a collective trust with one another.

When issues arose among them, most notably with Oliver, Stuart's trust (in Oliver's commitment to the team) was insufficient for eliminating the team's concerns. They did not share in Stuart's confidence or positive regard for their colleague.

On a fundamental level, the team and Stuart had conflicting views about trust. Where the team's trust in Stuart was built on a professional expectation—that he would ensure fluidity and collaboration to meet organizational goals—his trust in them was far more personal as one experiences with a friend. That is not the kind of trust one would expect with a work colleague.

While Stuart was correct that relationships are built on trust, his understanding of how to scale that as a leader was not. Even as issues mounted, he continued to develop his relationships out of friendship, believing in the other person and trusting them to do the right thing. He expected his team would do likewise.

Indicators of that expectation were evident in his hands-off management style.

To wit:

Stuart had trusted Oliver to appropriately team and communicate with the others. He trusted Oliver had the best of intentions for the organization. He trusted the team could work around what *he* considered idiosyncrasies in Oliver's behavior.

Stuart trusted the team could cope with direct requests by the board—that his involvement was superfluous. Conversely, he trusted the board, acting in the organization's best interests, would be respectful of the team.

Finally, Stuart expected the team to trust him. Whenever a member expressed doubt about a problem being addressed or shared a concern about the way things were being handled, Stuart would explicitly say, "Trust me," and then not provide any further support for the team member to do so.

The result of this misguided concept of trust was disastrous. Stuart felt betrayed by the team's failure to trust in him, and the team considered Stuart's seemingly blind trust to be an abdication in his responsibility as their leader.

Like many leaders, Stuart had built relationships believing they would lead to trust. But those efforts, particularly in a professional setting, do not develop into trust; instead, they yield likability.

While the team liked Stuart personally, a friend was not the role they needed or expected him to play. Ironically, as the group became increasingly displeased with Stuart's leadership, the domino effect eroded the personal friendships he'd fostered from the start.

Stuart felt hopeless and with little left to build upon.

Asking for trust is not a substitute for taking appropriate action. And, as previously mentioned, Stuart's understanding of workplace trust was misguided. Stuart did not need to build or ask for trust when things went awry. He needed to act. He needed to provide role clarity.

ROLE CLARITY

Stuart recognized his role as a leader would entail a primary focus on achieving the organizational goals and initiatives set in place by the board. He focused heavily on hiring the right people, bonding with them, and then getting out of their way as they got their jobs done. He believed autonomy was the key to success and that each team member would possess role clarity about their unique position. He didn't see his role in leading the team would extend much further than getting the right people working together and then stepping back, letting them do their job.

Stuart had indeed proved a fantastic recruiter. He'd identified and brought in talented and motivated individuals. As such, his team was made up of top performers. They were dedicated and gave far more than 100 percent on the job—working weekends and overtime without being asked.

As is typical of high achievers, his team also had high expectations. They aspired to create change individually and collectively. They were eager to strengthen their organization and were sure of what they could achieve. Stuart had helped to ignite that flame. But then, they felt their ability to do their job successfully was being compromised. They felt their hard work did not have the payoff it should.

This is a crucial point: Awakened Leaders—those who have become aware of their role and know how to manage their leadership in support of their teams and ultimately, the organizations in which they serve—recognize that their role is not to focus on the objectives but to focus on creating an environment in which their team can *succeed* in reaching those objectives.

Stuart didn't realize that the team would need his involvement to establish clear roles and expectations and determine and enforce role boundaries. He further lacked the skills, and possibly confidence, to fully assume that responsibility. When things went wrong, Stuart's default was to say, "Trust me."

Trust is not a save-all. It isn't the answer to a problem or a request for help. Instead, asking for trust indicates that something is missing—something is wrong.

CONFLICT MANAGEMENT

Stuart was prone to avoid conflict. He was uncomfortable managing tensions, particularly among others.

Instead, he favored building and preserving relationships. When things went awry, he sought to smooth over the rough spots. While healthy workplace relations are essential, avoiding conflict as a strategy for creating those relationships is shortsighted. This avoidance is exhibited in leaders who respond to complaints or issues of conflict by telling others to "just deal with it" or "let it go."

Stuart's conflict avoidance is evident in his reluctance to manage the issues with Oliver and his aversion to providing the team with a layer of protection from the board. He focused on *his* relationships with others. He trusted his team of high achievers to work things out among themselves. For him, the alternative would be to dictate their behavior (and roles)—something he was not inclined to do. He valued autonomy and had an aversion to inserting himself or controlling the team.

While accountability and self-direction are essential, autonomy is not the key to healthy leadership. Leaving conflict unaddressed does not improve workplace relations. It stifles constructive communication and allows problems to fester. Over time, unaddressed conflict serves to undermine trust and engender suspicion. It precedes other objectionable behaviors like gossip, rumors, claims of favoritism, and side-taking, all of which came to pass for Stuart and his team.

It can be tricky to know when an issue requires intervention. When team members request help or issues are forced to the surface, as when Stuart's team "ambushed" Oliver, the tension needs to be addressed, not quelled. At those critical moments, the energy is a force of nature.

Just as you might miss the building of tension before an earthquake or a volcanic eruption, it's possible to miss the tension as it develops on your team. Nevertheless, you cannot deny the destruction it causes or ignore the needs that arise in the aftermath. If you experienced an earthquake or volcanic eruption, you would likely focus on stabilization and reconstruction. You would look for those who need help and provide it to them. The same must be done when a team experiences chaos and disruption.

When Stuart learned that his team "ambushed" Oliver, he would have been better served to ask himself, "What can I do to remedy this situation?" or to ponder, "Why did my team act in this way?" and "Why did they not trust this was under control?" instead of shaming them for taking action.

Unfortunately, that was not what occurred. Rather than provide help or focus on ways to stabilize and rebuild his team, Stuart's reaction was to discredit those seeking to bring change.

Were this a natural disaster, Stuart's actions would have been equivalent to setting the remaining structures on fire. Stuart's preference toward conflict avoidance led him down the wrong path. His stance on conflict management was to put an end to the conflict rather than to address it.

Conflict doesn't come with an On/Off switch. You can't shame someone into feeling differently. Dismissing a conflict won't help to resolve the issue. If anything, it will more likely exacerbate the problems—to cause others to "double down" on their significance.

WHAT I FOUND

When I began work with Stuart and his team, the group was hungry for support. Most were eager to meet with me, and despite their intense schedule and heavy demands, they made ample time to share the full breadth of their experience and struggle.

They recounted stories and examples that, while not entirely about Stuart or his leadership, spoke to the gap in his awareness—the gap that kept him from being the leader they needed him to be. One director spoke through tears; several peppered the conversation with cursing and wild gestures. They were passionate people, and they'd been feeling cornered by their situation for too long.

Stuart, too, was earnest and open during our meeting. He understood the group wasn't happy, and he wasn't happy with them either. He told me that he was doing everything he could. He believed the problem stemmed more from the group and their lack of trust in him.

The stories I heard identified that a philosophy of "us versus them" had evolved. On one side, Stuart and Oliver. On the other, the remaining directors who were impacted by Oliver's actions and Stuart's nonchalance.

While each of these directors shared that they liked Stuart personally (he had, after all, befriended each of them), they no longer wanted him as their leader. The autonomy he had so generously bestowed upon them seemed to equate to his separation from dealing with their (team) issues. The group was frustrated and felt abandoned. Stuart's lack of role clarity left them exposed to not only Oliver but to the board. He undermined their ability to succeed while still holding them responsible for delivering in their roles.

That was part of Stuart's gap. Unable to see his role in damaging trust or his struggles in establishing healthy role clarity, he continued with a pattern that led to increasing conflict and tension—a pattern that threatened to undermine the whole team, as some members were entertaining their departure. The rest of Stuart's gap stemmed from his lack of skill in managing conflict.

Stuart didn't recognize his role as a leader would necessitate addressing tensions among the team, and more to the point, he was entirely out of his element when dealing with conflict. His solution was to ignore it—to hope it would go away or resolve itself.

I've come across countless leaders who share Stuart's discomfort and distaste for managing conflict, the objection to getting involved. The trend toward conflict avoidance is frightfully common. But conflict management is an essential role of a leader, and Stuart's team needed him to step in, not shut them down. Avoidance only creates more problems while still failing to resolve the original issues already in motion.

CHAPTER FOUR

GARY

Before being recruited as the Dean of Studies at a large Southern California university, Gary had successfully held leadership positions in higher education and administration. When he was recruited from out of state, he was the college's top candidate for the job due to his prior successes in preparing an institution for accreditation. The university needed someone with that expertise—someone who could lead them to the next level.

Before coming on board, Gary learned the department he would lead had a faculty of nearly 100 educators, many of whom held tenure. While that would be daunting, Gary was not new to working with educators or large departmental structures. He had worked in academia for more than a decade, always taking on more responsibility when the opportunity or need presented itself. Beyond that, Gary had successfully led two other institutions toward accreditation. He had the expertise and the confidence to fulfill the expectations of this new role.

The first step Gary was quick to identify was structural. This group of 100+ faculty and professors, covering multiple disciplines, would need to be divided into subgroups. The accreditation process would be grueling enough; doing it without a logical structure that lends itself to straightforward charting and data collection would be impossible.

Logistically, Gary saw that he could divide the department into three disciplines: therapeutic, education, and social sciences. That would create clarity in the research and reporting needed as the department built a case for accreditation. Gary's natural sense of role clarity allowed him to decipher the necessary organizational layout and to set the wheels of change in motion.

He knew the second step was to identify a division head for each of the three groups—someone who would be his next in command for each division. Collectively, their role would allow Gary to focus on the bigger goal of accreditation.

Gary shared his plans with the faculty. He explained the need to divide the department and create a new level of structure, and the opportunity it would create for them. He informed them of the basic requirements for becoming one of his division heads. They included full tenure, ongoing research and writing, demonstrated leadership, etc. Gary encouraged them, asking any interested and qualified faculty member to submit their interest in a formal proposal. He then took it a step further, soliciting recommendations from the faculty and inviting them to nominate their peers for consideration.

Over the following several weeks, Gary received about a dozen formal proposals and informal recommendations. Along with his associate dean—who'd been with the university for nearly two decades and knew the faculty members well—Gary began reviewing the candidates for the three division head roles.

Gary and the associate dean debated the qualities of each: the promise of leadership they possessed, their relationship to the faculty at large, their capacity for working collaboratively with one another, and their ability to support the work of the accreditation process.

Once the two had finished their collective assessment and review of the candidates, Gary excused the associate dean from the process. He believed it would be essential that he take sole responsibility for identifying the faculty who would fill the new roles. While to some, it appeared Gary was making a power play, trying to outshine the associate dean, his intention was to eliminate concerns of favoritism and bias. Gary felt certain his independent decision-making would allow the change to occur more seamlessly.

Gary understood the power and problems of tenure and the effort that a faculty member had to undertake to reach it—the competition that is created and the animosity it often caused. Gary knew that tenured faculty were often the most difficult for those holding administrative roles. They had power in the form of a permanent job contract, and they had deep roots in the form of relationships they'd forged along the way. He would ensure conflict was managed from the start by being the sole determiner of who filled the new roles.

Gary knew the third step of restructuring the department would be the most painful part of the process. He would be putting each division head in a position of authority over their newly formed group. Regardless of the quality of their relationship, he had determined who would report to whom. Gary knew the strain this would put on staff.

He expected some would be frustrated, others unhappy, and some potentially fearful. That was the impact of tenure. A permanent job with permanent colleagues meant that the quality of those relationships, good or bad, was magnified. Gary had a plan to remedy this. He would institute an open-door policy. Beyond creating an appropriate place for the faculty to bring their concerns, it would also be an excellent way for him to get to know them and build rapport.

Gary revealed his plan for restructuring to his newly appointed division heads first. He met with all three, identified the roles and responsibilities he intended for them to hold, and went over the changes that would be needed for reaching accreditation. He informed them of his expectation that they focus on the logistical aspects of managing the faculty—planning, course assignments, administrative needs, etc. And to clarify his understanding of tenure, he surfaced the idea that the new structure would create tension for several faculty members, perhaps even the three of them. He went on to say that he had a plan for that.

To alleviate the potential for friction, he would be responsible for managing the people issues. He shared his intention to create an open-door policy so members of the faculty could come to him directly to share their concerns or simply speak with him. He explained that this would alleviate the burden on them. Their role would be hard enough, he said. The division heads weren't sure but accepted Gary's plan. One less thing to worry about seemed okay to them.

Once Gary had shared the plans with his division heads, the time had come for rolling out the information to the rest of the department. He held a kickoff meeting where he laid out the full breadth of changes to the faculty. Gary was intentional in his process. He knew it wouldn't be easy, but he was sure it was possible. He was taking steps to establish trust and develop clear roles. And he had developed a plan to address tensions before they erupted into conflict.

Gary met with the whole faculty group and clarified the divisional breakdown and reporting structure. He explained that the teams were delineated based on the courses taught and that, in turn, determined to whom each would report. He added that for those members who crossed over more than one area of discipline, he decided which team they would report to strategically to create a balance between the divisions in terms of numbers and demographics.

Next, Gary laid out his expectations. He explained that each division would have the responsibility of compiling data and reports, each division head would be responsible for ensuring timeliness and accuracy, each group would need to be housed closely together to facilitate easy dialogue and collaboration, and the division heads would be responsible for determining course schedules and instruction.

EARLY COMPLAINTS

As Gary had anticipated, there was immediate dissension. Upon learning of the changes, members began to voice concerns. Gary took the opportunity to inform the group of his open-door policy, which several made quick use of—some over personal concerns, others logistical matters.

Personal concerns went beyond the discomfort of change. Some faculty members came to Gary worried about the authority these new division heads would wield, especially the power to determine course dispersion. They were concerned about their division head's ability to effectively bench them, giving away teaching courses they'd long possessed, impacting their income and workload.

Other faculty members took issue directly with Gary's particular selection of division heads. While each newly appointed leader had measured up to the required elements and held high accolades in their respective field, their different personality types, work styles, and interpersonal relations became the focus of concern.

Some faculty members boldly approached Gary to suggest he'd made the wrong selection. They didn't trust Gary had made the right call. They pointed out that he, being new to the university, was unfamiliar with the shortcomings each possessed. While agreeing to hear their concerns, Gary felt confident of his decision and held his ground. The roles he had put in place made sense. They would support accreditation. Besides, his plan for managing conflict was working; people were coming to him. He was sure it would all blow over—that things would settle down and reach a place of stability. He was wrong.

Over the coming months, complaints intensified, mainly about two of the three division heads: Andrew, the head of the Therapeutic Division, and Berniece, head of the Education Division. While the two were similar on paper, they were vastly different in action, and their teams felt it.

As a part of their role and their responsibility for determining course offerings and scheduling the faculty instructors, each division head was charged with holding a monthly meeting with their group and collecting data and reports from the faculty essential for supporting the accreditation process.

Berniece brought structure and a goal-oriented approach as she took on her role. Her team meetings were mandatory. The reports were to be on time. She had guidelines for just about everything.

Berniece took her role and the responsibilities of getting things done very seriously. If a member of her division could not attend a meeting or get their reports in on time, she was clear that their teaching schedules and course assignments could be adjusted to ensure they would have the time necessary. Berniece wasn't trying to build trust or form new relationships. This was a job, and she knew her role. Berniece was seen as a strong leader by her closest colleagues and friends. She was seen as a dictatorial tyrant by those who lacked positive and historical rapport.

Andrew ran his group far differently. He believed his division of accomplished adults could be trusted to get things done. He held meetings but allowed others to contribute to the agenda or lead a discussion. He reminded them of reporting deadlines but was not overly concerned if a member told him they would be sending him things a day or two late. Andrew had a relaxed style that was fitting of his therapeutic roots, and most everyone who reported to him liked being in his division.

Complaints, however, surfaced about both division heads. Those reporting to Berniece complained about her intensity and authoritarian manner. They referenced her heavy-handedness and compared it unfavorably to Andrew's more relaxed style.

The complaints arising from Andrew's division came, not surprisingly, from the faculty with a solid connection to Berniece. In support of Berniece, they challenged Andrew's ability to properly manage their group, collect reports, or get other things done on time. The vocal members of the Therapeutic Division specifically called out Gary for having decided to promote Andrew. They were quick to remind Gary of the goal being accreditation. They challenged the notion that Andrew had the competency to help get it done.

Gary listened but chalked the issues up as a settling-in period. Things would calm down. He kept his open-door policy in place to hear all the issues his team brought to him but did not make changes to the division leadership.

Beyond the personality differences, Gary was getting complaints arising from logistical concerns. When he split the department into three groups, Gary intended to create a degree of uniformity, balance, and order. That extended beyond academic instruction to workspaces and office locations, committee appointments, and so on. To create the balance essential for accreditation, Gary had known that shifts in the original distribution of these elements would be needed.

Once the faculty members were assigned to their respective divisions, many of those needs became apparent. Specifically, Gary quickly noticed that most of the opportunities for advancement within the entire department leaned heavily into the Education Division. Similarly, most of the funding within the department was going toward that division. As a result, Berniece's group boasted newer technology, a more extensive administrative staff, more interns, etc. The reason was clear; those in the Education Division were like Berniece—competitive go-getters.

Before Gary's arrival or the university's interest in seeking accreditation for the department, those faculty members had actively pursued grant funding, special projects, and volunteered to be on committees. Before the department was divided, the imbalance was unimportant. After it was divided, however, given the scrutinous eye of accreditation, it needed to change.

Gary attended to this imbalance as he had the other changes, as a well-meaning vigilante.

He redistributed some of the funding. He made modifications to committee appointments. He added or removed people from upcoming projects. Gary saw himself as a benevolent dictator. He made the changes in the name of the greater good. But he often did so without first discussing it with those who would be affected. Indeed, without a full appreciation for the impact it would create.

Because Berniece's group members were most often these go-getters, members of the Education Division were disproportionately affected by the changes.

In his haste to create balance, Gary overlooked the fact that it would be unfair to those who had worked tirelessly on funding proposals or had lobbied long and hard to be on a special committee. He gave little concern that many were coveted committee appointments, which held a constructive element in a faculty member's bid for tenure. Gary only saw the big picture. He imagined the team would trust him and his judgment for making these changes. The use of his open-door policy and the number of complaints he was receiving suggested otherwise.

Gary had come on board as the Dean of Studies to ready the department for accreditation. He knew it was his responsibility to identify and make sweeping changes, even if they were not well-liked or received. The substantive changes he made were an inevitability. Without them, accreditation would not be possible. Now, though, Gary had several faculty making efforts to meet with him over his changes.

MANAGING THE COMPLAINTS

True to his word, Gary listened to the complaints of the faculty when they came to discuss their concerns or frustration with the changes he had been making. He made time for them and listened intently to their concerns. Often, and to his surprise, he found himself agreeing with them as they asserted an issue.

Gary was interested in making things right. However, his efforts at conflict management were shortsighted. Gary made consequential mistakes in his attempt to manage the complaints.

It began modestly when one faculty member met with Gary to privately point out that a senior faculty member had *not* moved his office as had been required as part of restructuring the department into separate divisions. The professor who had ignored this requirement was a part of the Therapeutic Division, but his office—one of the biggest on the floor—remained in a central location of the Education Division. With fairness issues and complaints already rising, the faculty member pointed out that allowing anyone to maintain a large office in the other group's section was inappropriate. Beyond the fairness issue, this faculty member asserted, given the complaints already circulating about committee appointments, and the selection of division heads, allowing that professor to retain his office location was likely to create opportunities for eavesdropping and could give way to gossip.

Gary got the point. He agreed to engage with the professor about moving his office.

The faculty member had one other concern to discuss. While the open-door policy allowed her to come to Gary, she wanted anonymity. She was concerned about being identified as having made the complaint. That professor, she knew, would not be happy about the requirement to move. And tenure being what it is, she was certain to be working closely with the professor and his friends for the balance of her career.

Her request for anonymity was not the first. It was consistent among many faculty members who brought their concerns to Gary's attention.

Gary respected the individuals who approached him and listened intently to their concerns. As he saw it, the problems they brought forth were rarely raised out of self-interest. Some were in defense of a friend or colleague, others seemingly to support the mission of getting the department accredited. Gary wanted to encourage their helpful guidance and agreed to eliminate the fears attached. Each time a member approached Gary with a concern, he assured that person confidentiality.

Confidentiality as such became inextricably linked to Gary's open-door policy. However, Gary neglected to consider that confidentiality is a double-edged sword. It can undermine trust just as easily as it can support it.

Being the self-proclaimed benevolent dictator, Gary was unafraid to address things head-on and make the adjustments he saw fit. He had the seasoned professor move his office, and he made other changes based on information shared during the open-door, confidential meetings.

Understandably, the faculty began to ask questions. Why were these changes being made? Who had made a complaint about the situation? Indeed, someone must have complained!

True to his word, Gary kept everything confidential. When more and more questions were brought to him, his mantra became the simple expression, "Trust me."

For Gary, all the changes were purposeful, strategic, related to the organizational needs, and essential for attaining accreditation. But beneath the surface, a very different story was beginning to take shape.

To the faculty, a pattern of secrecy and change was emerging where "trust me" was replacing honest conversations. The suppression of information was felt most painfully by those adversely affected by the changes—primarily those in the Education Division. In the Education Division, which had already been disproportionately impacted by the redistribution of funding and shifting of committee appointments, more "adjustments" were being made. Each was a direct result of the clandestine meetings with Gary.

Frustrated and uninformed, members of the Education Division began to voice their concerns, not with Gary, but privately, within small, trusted circles. Behind closed doors, questions and theories began to emerge.

- What was behind these changes?
- Who's been talking—*complaining*—to Gary?
- Why has the Therapeutic Division been handed so many plum opportunities and committee positions?
- Why did Gary give a pass to the Therapeutic Division when their reports were late?

It didn't take long for members of the Education Division to conclude that Gary was demonstrating favoritism for Andrew and the Therapeutic Division.

Once that idea was voiced, the group began to gossip and share information. They began to look for evidence that supported their suspicions. Trust, already damaged, was rapidly eroding.

This is a common phenomenon and happens when there is a vacuum of information. As humans, we seek to make sense of our world. When the details are insufficient to create logic and understanding, we try to fill those gaps.

The problem is, in our haste to make sense of our world, we are not overly concerned with finding the correct answer. Instead, we take shortcuts and look for evidence to support our suspicions. The amateur investigator sleuthing to confirm his ideas doesn't recognize or perhaps care that the "proof" he is collecting may be faulty or circumstantial.

Think of the crime dramas you've seen. The story intensifies as the police or detectives find a lead that puts everything in order. The case seems solved within the first ten minutes. But soon, other evidence turns up. While we were ready to close the case, the detectives had continued searching. They do this because they understand circumstantial evidence is of limited value; knowing a fingerprint at the crime scene allows us to infer that the fingerprint and the crime are connected. But just as we see when the story's drama unfolds, the two events are not related in the way we imagined. The cause-and-effect conclusion we reached using the evidence we had was incorrect. Most of us believe we are great detectives, but how often do we continue our sleuthing beyond that first piece of evidence?

As expected, the Education Division team found evidence to support their suspicions. It was in part because they spent little, if any, time looking for evidence that would refute it. Through their conjecture, the group became certain of Gary's favoritism for Andrew.

Things escalated as some of the team's guesswork turned out to be accurate. As they correctly predicted who had made a complaint or requested a change, they became even more emboldened in their assertions that foul play was at hand. However, the accuracy of their sleuthing led to an even more profound issue. The spillover effect. Now, those who had engaged in confidential meetings with Gary suddenly felt exposed, but they didn't know who had exposed them. They trusted Gary had kept their meetings confidential. They also knew with whom, if anyone, *they* had shared their concerns.

That gave rise to more questions, and it gave rise to fear. Who was leaking this information? How did *that person* learn of it? Was it the product of eavesdropping, or did someone break confidentiality? Who stood to benefit from the information being exposed?

Suspicions began to run rampant. They ranged from considerations that someone had, serendipitously or not, seen them leaving Gary's office, to believing the office and support staff were involved, to a belief that they were the victims of outright spying. Everyone involved was observing the others, each suspicious act adding to the already rising speculation about who was involved—who was spreading gossip. Not surprisingly, the more these rumors and whispers left faculty feeling fearful or exposed, the more Gary's office was being sought for confidential meetings. The lack of trust he created evolved into a vicious and intensifying cycle.

As the suspicion and gossip intensified, other problems took root within the department. Those within the Education Division became increasingly insular. Rather than guessing who was safe to speak to or risk being accused of spying or spreading rumors, those faculty closest to the Education Division head, Berniece, kept their conversations close. Their fear that Gary favored Andrew caused them to limit their interactions and conversations.

Faculty deemed "outsider" members of the Education Division (those known to maintain a close relationship with Andrew and the Therapeutic Division team) became effectively ostracized.

In turn, the excluded group sought refuge in the only place they felt safe—with Andrew and his team. As each gravitated toward safety, the two divisions became polarized along personal and social lines.

All Things Circle Back to Trust — a Side Note about Gary and His Team

Life doesn't always unfold in the ways we plan. As I presented the growing conflict brewing in Gary's department, I left out part of the story. Gary, too, kept information hidden as he led his team to accreditation, but we'll soon see it was a pivotal detail.

When Gary first relocated to Southern California, he and his wife had no friends or connections in their community. Gary, a longtime member of Toastmasters, joined the local chapter. In it, he made a new acquaintance, Lou, and the two men quickly became close friends. They introduced their spouses, and in a short time, the four friends became inseparable. They spent time together and frequently included one another in their social planning.

But that new friendship was a closely guarded secret. Lou, it turns out, was married to Andrew, the professor cum division leader in Gary's department.

Even though Gary and Lou had not yet met when the department was divided and division heads selected, Andrew knew it could be a problem. The divisiveness in the department was sure to get worse if this were revealed. Andrew implored Gary to keep their personal connection private, to which Gary agreed.

Out of an abundance of caution, Andrew maintained a distance from Gary at the university. He kept problems to himself and avoided using Gary's open-door policy. He knew the potential for impropriety was tremendous and was determined to steer clear of it.

Gary was aware of Andrew's reluctance to approach him with problems. He understood it was to keep their professional relationship clean and separate from their personal friendship. However, Gary heard the gossip and rumors firsthand. Some of it specifically targeted Andrew, suggesting he (Andrew) had been the instigator of complaints or that he was the one behind all the requests from which his team was benefiting. Gary wanted to openly defend Andrew, but out of respect for Andrew, he showed restraint.

Regardless of their efforts to keep a professional distance and operate with the highest level of integrity, details of their friendship still came out. A chance occurrence involving a member of the

Education Division brought the information to light. Before either Gary or Andrew was even aware of the discovery, the gossip of their connection was beginning to spread.

As Gary and Andrew did, one could argue that the relationship doesn't matter because both men had truly set it aside. If anything, Andrew could claim that he made less effort to garner support from Gary for himself or his team. Even when there was merit for calling upon Gary's influence, he had avoided doing so. Andrew was careful to ensure there could be no indiscretion, real or imagined. Gary could say the same and attest that he made no concessions for Andrew. But those arguments are shortsighted. By keeping their friendship a secret, Gary and Andrew made it impossible for others to trust them. It called the legitimacy of their friendship into question. It undermined the already weakened trust in the department.

Gary and Andrew failed to consider that trust is strengthened or weakened by every interaction we have. Their discretion for sharing, however purposeful, sabotaged their intentions.

While the two men believed their friendship could be kept private if they acted with the utmost propriety, they couldn't have been more wrong. Because Gary and Andrew hid it, their secrecy provided "proof" of favoritism for those who had already suspected it.

Those faculty rightly asked, "Why keep a secret if everything is legitimate?" Making matters worse, the information had come to light without either Gary or Andrew knowing. Their innocent secret and the doubt it created quickly spread like wildfire.

But this was all happening behind the scenes.

As the complaints increased and the silos between the Education and Therapeutic Divisions were becoming formidable, Gary felt frustrated and put-upon. All the gossip, all the complaints—where were they coming from? Who was behind it?

It wasn't long before Gary was as given to suspicion as the rest of the team. His concern, however, was more specific. He was alarmed at the lapses in confidentiality. Not only was it causing damage within his department, but confidentiality was also a tenet *taught* by this department. The reputation of the entire group was at stake. How deep did these problems reach? How much damage was being done?

Gary tried to isolate the issues and determine who was breaching confidentiality, spreading gossip and rumors. What did he know? He knew *he* had not broken confidentiality. He had fiercely maintained it. He was keeping things quiet and protecting those who had come to him. Yet, information was still spreading.

Some gossip and false accusations were brought directly to Gary during his open-door meetings. He saw that many of the issues could be traced back to members of Berniece's division.

It didn't take long before things began adding up. Berniece's team members were the biggest complainers of the change. They'd lost the most—a complaint he heard often. The gossip and rumors commonly targeted Andrew or a member of his Therapeutic Division.

Gary found himself unable to stay balanced or impartial. Given his trust and friendship with Andrew, all of this was becoming too much to bear. Gary became more aligned with Andrew's therapeutic group, distanced and untrusting of Berniece and her supporters.

It had to stop. Gary couldn't lead like that. He couldn't fulfill his role in bringing about accreditation. The department was falling apart, and he had to put an end to it. Gary held an all-faculty meeting, wanting to end the cycle of gossip and rumor. Rather than getting into the weeds and starting from the beginning to explain the decisions or rationale behind his changes, he attempted to refocus the group on the future and their common goal—accreditation.

Many of his staff bristled as Gary glossed over the tensions of the prior months.

But Gary was unwilling to break anyone's confidences or delve into the conflict and complaints. He didn't believe it would help, and he certainly didn't want to discuss it. He implored the staff, "Trust me." He expected them to move on.

It was too late. They knew too much, including their "proof" of Gary's favoritism toward Andrew. That piece of gossip had already been circulating among Berniece's group. Rather than trust Gary, moving on as he had implored, they took matters into their own hands. They attempted to undermine Andrew by starting rumors of an affair.

Far from stopping, the rumors and gossip were becoming more personal, more damaging. As things continued to deteriorate, Gary reached his breaking point. He drew a proverbial line in the sand. He insisted the behaviors stop, and in a group meeting, said, "You're either with me, or you're against me."

Gary had intended for that statement to refocus the team on their shared goal of working together—of completing the accreditation process. But to all those familiar with the tension between the two divisions, it seemed clear he was stating his allegiance to Andrew and his team. To them, the rumor of favoritism was prominent and undeniable. Gary's words echoed like a confession. They felt both vindicated and afraid. The rumor of favoritism was now a reality.

FINDING THE GAP — THE LEADER'S ABYSS

Do Gary's story and the way things unfolded leave you somewhat perplexed? I imagine you feel you're lacking a clear picture of what went wrong or what exactly needed to change. It was certainly true for those involved at the university. Even as an expert called upon to help address the issues and restore healthy workplace relations, it took me weeks to dissect not only what was happening but why and how to change it.

Solving a situation of this magnitude, one with so many people involved, each pointing a finger in another direction, is much like completing a challenging jigsaw puzzle or solving a complicated game of Sudoku. There are many variables. You may think you see a solution, but then the pieces don't quite fit together. Making an error in one part of the puzzle undermines your ability to solve the rest.

Rather than walk you through all the possibilities and assumptions uncovered, I'm going to shine a light on the real problems I identified—those that needed to be fixed.

Like most of the leaders I have encountered, and certainly all of those in this book, Gary is a good person who had good intentions. A self-proclaimed benevolent dictator, Gary believed he was serving the department well by protecting the faculty. He took responsibility for making the hard decisions while also shielding others from blame. Even as he felt concerned about how things were transpiring, Gary believed his goodness and intentions would see him through. He also believed that the end (regardless of what happened in the interim) would justify the means.

Like Stuart, Gary's leadership was impacted by issues of:

- Trust
- Role Clarity
- Conflict Management

TRUST

Gary experienced a feeling of urgency when he came on board as dean at the university. He had a timeline and knew he had to work swiftly to get things moving toward accreditation. A lot would need to happen, and in his effort to quickly build the support he needed, Gary tried to take a shortcut. Rather than put in the work to build trust as the leader of the team, he was given to asserting a simple directive to the department: "Trust me."

Gary didn't give much consideration to the fact that he was new and had not established any real credibility with the faculty—that while he had the authority to make decisions, it takes time to develop the trust needed for making substantial changes. Gary lacked the trust and support a leader needs to seamlessly divide the department, determine who will head each division, shift committee appointments, and require people to move their offices. While he saw himself as the benevolent dictator, others experienced him as more of a bull in a china shop.

Still, Gary moved forward. He not only made impactful changes, but he also did so independently, unilaterally, and often in isolation of others' input. When making decisions, he purposefully dismissed his associate dean and later his self-appointed division heads. His reasoning was clear: this would prevent the faculty from internal discord. But it was ultimately his undoing. Gary had not recognized the impact his actions would have on others or how his decisions, made privately, would lead to questions and doubts. He hadn't realized that his actions brought about the opposite of what he was seeking. His efforts led to distrust.

Lack of trust was the fundamental issue impacting Gary's leadership and ultimately his team. But other factors stacked on top of that core concern, each further compromising Gary's leadership and the team.

Ironically, the tactics that undermined Gary's leadership and disintegrated trust were related to his strategies for building a relationship with his team: his open-door policy, the promise of confidentiality, and his commitment to being responsible for all people issues. All these led to more significant issues of conflict. In particular, the ownership of people issues is a misstep related to role clarity.

ROLE CLARITY

Gary's conception of role clarity stretched only as far as the separation of duties he'd instituted. Division heads would be responsible for academic planning, course dispersion, curriculum planning, and general management of the faculty. Gary would be responsible for leading the department, guiding the accreditation process, making decisions, and managing all people issues. Gary wanted to be responsible for managing the faculty, ensuring they got along and that decisions were made fairly and equitably.

Accustomed to bonding quickly with others, Gary felt confident in his ability to manage the people issues. Being new to the area, he was interested in forming new relationships. He wanted to meet and connect with the faculty. However, Gary neglected to recognize the value and purpose of having a chain of command.

Each time Gary invited faculty members to meet with him and share their concerns, he undermined his division heads. He thought nothing of it. As he saw it, that was his role. He compounded this mistake by engaging in promises and commitments such as those about committee appointments and office locations, which should have remained outside of his purview.

Gary took those actions without informing his division heads or soliciting their input.

By leaving the division heads out of the loop, Gary blindsided his next in command. Those leaders only learned of a change after the fact, when a team member would come to them with a complaint or concern about the changes afoot. The division heads were being undermined and found themselves unable to stop the problems at their source. Gary made the changes, firmly held to them, and refused to engage with them about it.

Mind you, the division heads were not especially interested in this responsibility. Some were glad to be relieved of the drama. But all of them became frustrated at managing the chaos left in the wake of Gary's decision-making. They experienced a growing lack of control over their teams and the situation.

Gary's view of himself as the benevolent dictator blinded him to the reality that his actions led to conflict and confusion. He had a good heart, a sound mind, and good intentions. Unfortunately, his interpretation of role clarity and his understanding of building trusting relationships were sorely lacking. Rather than solving or preventing issues, Gary's rogue processes and lack of role clarity throughout the department spawned a growing number of conflicts.

CONFLICT MANAGEMENT

Gary lacked a clear strategy for managing conflict. From his perspective, conflict would be best managed and contained if one unbiased person handled it. He instituted an open-door policy and made himself the hub for all complaints with the intent of circumventing potential conflicts and eliminating concerns of side-taking. Gary ensured confidentiality with the plan of preventing gossip and back-channel discussions. He took responsibility for the people issues, believing this would allow everyone to work fluidly, trusting that conflicts would be minimized or eliminated. Unfortunately, Gary was wrong.

Open-Door Policy and Confidentiality

Gary thought his open-door policy would support his role as the leader. He would strengthen his knowledge and connection with the faculty. He would resolve their issues and, by keeping their concerns and complaints confidential, he would form relationships built on trust.

But Gary didn't recognize the true purpose of an open-door policy: to enhance information sharing, build broader awareness, and support collaborative planning. Gary's open-door policy stood in stark contrast to those ideals. As the sole point of contact, he impeded any broad awareness. By making decisions unilaterally, there was no opportunity for collaborative planning. Gary incorporated the policy so that he would be the hub of all information—so he could attend to tensions and determine how disagreements were managed. He went into it with the right intentions, but the plan quickly showed its flaws.

Reasonably, staff felt concerned about the information they were sharing with Gary and how it would be handled. He was new to them, to the university. The concerns they were bringing forward could put them in a precarious position if made public. To remedy this, Gary coupled his open-door policy with a commitment to confidentiality. With that added element, Gary believed he would satisfy the needs of the faculty. He would have their trust. But Gary's now-enhanced open-door policy not only lacked in building collaboration and awareness, it also shrouded information behind a veil of secrecy. That added element effectively eliminated information sharing.

Given all the secrecy and changes, questions and concerns quickly and understandably arose from the faculty. Gary presumed the changes would just take time. The faculty would adjust. He forged ahead with the same plan—being the hub and decision-maker, protecting his team from exposure. Gary erroneously believed he could eliminate their concerns and shoulder the responsibility for any changes by simply telling them, "Trust me."

Gary neglected to consider that those impacted would not be so easily appeased, that they would need an explanation, that they would want and deserve to know the reasons behind the changes affecting them, and that in the absence of clear information, they would be given to anger, doubt, and suspicion. Gary's keeping his commitment to confidentiality and responding to concerns with "trust me" did the opposite of what he intended. Gary didn't build trust; he created fear and doubt.

Favoritism

The confidentiality created a vacuum. It left others to come up with their own explanation for what was happening and why. Some who had expressed their views early on suggested Andrew was less competent than Berniece—that he shouldn't be a division leader. Those vocal opponents to his selection noted that others were more deserving, more competent. Already fueled with suspicion, those faculty members soon saw committee changes and funding transfers that consistently benefited Andrew's Therapeutic Division. It was an easy conclusion to draw: Andrew was being favored.

Once the idea was floated, more and more "evidence" seemed to solidify it. Circumstantial or not, the group's confirmation bias led them to trust the information as fact, fueling more rumors and creating greater discord.

Gary knew he was not playing favorites. He'd selected Andrew as a division head *before* they had formed a personal connection. His shifts in committee appointments and funding were done to create the balance needed for accreditation. Even so, Gary wasn't one to stoop to the level of defending his decision or actions. He was the leader. It was just noise. He decided to ignore what he saw as sophomoric behavior, believing that the team would see, over time, that his choices were for the best.

Andrew, likewise, chose to stay out of the fray. He willingly kept a low profile, maintained distance, and rarely approached Gary with any questions or needs. Both men believed the issues would subside and calm down. They thought they could rise above it. It didn't work.

Rather than be quelled by the lack of attention to their claims, it caused greater suspicion for some faculty. Their belief that favoritism was fueling the changes going on in the department caused them to speculate further.

If the two didn't interact on campus, they must meet off campus or talk outside of business hours. The belief that there were secrets between the two men was reaching a fevered pitch.

Even as the chaos heightened, Gary did not change course. He remained convinced that he was avoiding conflict in keeping decisions to himself. He was merely keeping confidences and protecting those who had come to him. By refusing to engage, Gary saw that he could sidestep any discussion about his connection with Andrew more easily.

Unfortunately, Gary didn't realize that his silence and refusal to engage about his decisions was fueling the rumors and conflict, not dispelling them. The ensuing fear was leading to the formation of protective silos.

WHAT I FOUND

When I was brought on board, conflict issues were inundating the department of this Southern California university. The complaints were overwhelming both departmental leaders and the university's Human Resources department. They were in desperate need of help, wanting to unravel and resolve the conflicts afoot so they could restore order and function to the department.

Upon working with this group, I immediately got a sense of the chaos. Initially described as a conflict between two division leaders (Andrew and Berniece) and their respective supporters, it quickly became clear that the issues stemmed elsewhere. Far too many faculty members were looking to speak with me, to be heard, and share their stories and conclusions. Identifying the core issues was not easy.

While I find this true of many conflicts and team issues, the breadth and depth of this department's problems were far more confounding. I felt like Alice in Wonderland with the faculty and administrative leaders collectively taking on the role of the Cheshire cat, each unwittingly pointing me in the wrong direction.

Being accustomed to the noise of differing ideas, I listened attentively while tuning out the distractions, finger-pointing, and blame. Still, it took nearly two dozen interviews, analyzed collectively, before I could see the big picture. While most of the faculty had homed in on Andrew, Berniece, or their respective supporters as the source of the problems, I narrowed in on Gary.

It was clear that Gary, like many leaders, had positive intentions. He was purposeful in his organization of the department. He instituted well-meaning policies. However, Gary had not fully considered the ramifications of his choices.

The professional roles Gary delineated for himself and his division heads created the first problem. While formed to build clarity, define responsibility, and eliminate the possibility of favoritism, the duties were inappropriately skewed. The structure granted Gary the authority to interfere while holding him immune from responsibility.

The second problem was born out of Gary's attempts to build trust and rapport. Gary had encouraged faculty to meet with him and to discuss their concerns. He created an open-door policy to support the effort. He was successful in that the faculty came to him readily, but the result did not build trust so much as it created coconspirators. The faculty trusted Gary, but they did not trust one another.

The third problem arose as Gary sought to assure the faculty cum coconspirators that they were safe and their conversations with him private. Gary agreed to keep those discussions confidential. He saw protecting those who met with him as part of his strategy for managing conflict. Instead, the secrecy led to suspicions. It became the linchpin of the conflicts that erupted.

For all his efforts in establishing roles, creating trust, and managing conflict, Gary instead found himself surrounded by conflict, claims of favoritism, and growing silos. His faculty members were left experiencing deepening fear and an inability to trust anyone beyond their closest allies. Gary did not know how he or the team got there. He remained certain that it was nefarious influencers within his own department. Gary did not see that he was responsible. Like many leaders, he was blind to his gap.

CHAPTER FIVE

JOSEPHINE

Josephine was passionate and dedicated. She loved the organization where she worked, and she was deeply committed to its success. Working in support of movie-making and other aspects of the film industry was exciting. While some thought her passion was tied to the thrill of being connected, however fringe, to the entertainment industry, Josephine knew better. Her commitment wasn't about glitz, glamour, or the promise of a career in lights. Those weren't within reach, even if they had been her interest. No; for Josephine, it was about people working together and building something of purpose. She loved the company because she felt her growth was a part of its growth. She had been on board when it all began. While the company now boasted nearly 350 employees, she was one of the original five. More than twenty years had passed, and she still held a visceral memory of those first few years—the struggle, the shoestring budget, the uncertainty of its future.

When it all began, Josephine and the other four initial hires were all young in their careers. During the interview process, each had been informed that the company's seed funding was only enough to sustain the business for six months. They learned that no additional funding would come without demonstrated success, and then they would all be out of a job. The newly formed team recognized it wasn't a threat; it was a reality. They were being forewarned that it was going to be an uphill battle.

Josephine and the others were undaunted. The threat almost became a joke among them, teasing one another. "You better keep your resume up to date," or "You better step it up, or the business could close."

The do-or-die challenge established a shared commitment among the small team: their tenuous start generated camaraderie. The genuine teamwork that resulted from those early days may well have been the key to the organization's success.

The original team was a confident bunch, each believing in themselves and their abilities. They trusted the others, shared their commitment, and held a similar inner strength. All five were excited to jump in and hit the ground running. They were eager to do whatever it took to make the business a success. The shared commitment dictated the team's behavior. They routinely pitched in, asked for help when needed, communicated openly, and shared information readily. They displayed teamwork at its best.

While each was hired to fill a particular role complete with specific goals and tasks, the overarching importance of helping the business to thrive (so that they would all still have a job in six months) dictated their behavior. When a team member recognized their load was light, they were quick to offer help and assist another member. When several felt inundated at once, they rallied to support one another. They kept each other's spirits high. They laughed, struggled, overcame, and succeeded as a unit.

Due to their propensity to pitch in and their crossover responsibilities, each became well versed in the roles of the others. Each of the five took more responsibility and ownership than was expected—never less. And each showed gratitude to the others for their dedication and commitment to make it work. Their attitude and behavior were the epitome of healthy teamwork. Trusting they had the support of their team, each soared with confidence.

Not surprisingly, given their commitment, the team and business survived the six-month mark. They had achieved more than anyone expected. By rolling up their sleeves in support of one another, the originating team successfully developed the initial structure and foundation for the business as it began to grow.

Over the following two years, the business grew and developed roots. It became apparent the company had the potential to survive long-term.

New employees were hired who reported to the original five. In turn, the initiating team was given upgraded titles, roles, and distinct responsibilities.

All five original team members remained on board and were excited to train their small, newly formed team. They were determined to recreate the magic that worked so well for them. They mentored their new hires on both the work and how to perform well in concert with the rest of the team. Even as Josephine and her four colleagues began their evolution into more distinct and specific roles, they remained committed to maintaining the intertwined nature of their work. Each understood and valued the importance of the teamwork they had formed.

Still a fledgling business operation, there was a newly formed second layer of staff. Though the original five were given no training on how to develop their teams or manage others, they muddled through much as before, with grit and determination. They wanted to infuse their new group with the same enthusiasm, energy, teamwork, and dedication they held when they began to work at the company. But with more people on staff, roles had to become more distinct. While the original group instilled the importance of teamwork and overlapping effort, there were signs that role clarity was becoming an issue.

Over the next decade, the business continued to grow along with an increase in staffing. At seven years, it jumped to fifty employees, and five years later leaped to one hundred fifty. Three of the original five company hires, including Josephine, remained on board, each now holding the position of director. Two others were hired along the way and were elevated to join their ranks. But the effortless harmony of those earlier days was gone. The rationale behind a commitment or decision was no longer immediately apparent to the whole team.

Back then, it was easy to collaborate and discuss the circumstances at hand. They were all intimately involved in the decisions that impacted their work. Each had clarity on what was expected of them and why it was needed. Now, that connection to the impact on each other and the big picture was far less clear. While there was greater role clarity, there was a dimming awareness of how all the pieces fit together.

Josephine and the other directors, who had been aboard since the organization's genesis, maintained their long-held commitment to ensure its survival. All three were knowledgeable and capable across many aspects of the business. They could foresee a shifting in the workload before it was apparent to the newer directors. They were so well versed in what was needed, that they continued to support each other without being asked, providing staff and resources where a need arose. It was almost seamless. Almost.

As young leaders, each director was eager to carve out a strong career. But the vision each had of how to get there was different. While all five, by necessity, interacted primarily within their individual teams, the two directors who had recently risen through the ranks developed an entirely inward focus. Far from sharing the philosophies of "all for one and one for all" or "together we shall all succeed" (ideals still held by the original members), these newer directors were looking out for the best interests of their groups and the individuals within them. The once high-level appreciation for the interdependent nature of the work and its impact on the other teams had faded. The once core value of teamwork was morphed into a more insular form.

Unlike those early years, when the crossover was fluid, each of the current directors and their respective teams now had distinct responsibilities. Their objectives had become clearly laid out in job descriptions and performance reports. Yet, just as in the early days, there remained considerable overlap and interdependency in their activities. The research that one team provided determined the services another would recommend, a third would schedule, and a fourth would perform. Multiple groups were involved in every deliverable the client would see. The goal was still for the work to appear seamless, but the challenge became more pronounced because the teams were no longer unified, and communication was no longer fluid.

The change was unavoidable, and the original three members knew it. When a business has several teams, each engaged in performing their own set of functions, they are expected to lean on each other, not members of a separate group in the organization. They recognize the need to pitch in and help members within their group or team but not beyond it. Silos will naturally develop, and an us-versus-them mentality will inevitably grow, further separating the teams. So was the case at Josephine's company.

Josephine's team was the most connected to the clients and was central to the organization; so, she felt the transformation pointedly. With the teams disjointed, her work was slowed. She or her team often had to circle back to the other groups multiple times. She knew things weren't working.

Experience told her that the interdependence of those teams remained critical and that to lose it would cripple the organization. She instinctively began to transform her role.

Well-liked and with a strong connection to the other directors, Josephine took steps to bring change. She asked all the team leaders to run information by her. Being clear of the client's wants and needs, she sped up the work as she quickly identified problems and determined solutions. Understanding the workflow, she could see when things needed to be redirected and could appropriately influence the decision-making process. Her fellow directors, especially the two who had been with her from the earliest days, appreciated her involvement. It sped things up. It reignited the sense of teamwork that had been lost.

It became clear that Josephine was unmatched in her capacity to understand the organizational priorities and day-to-day operational needs. She knew the integral role each team played in running the business. The team trusted her wisdom, followed her leadership. As a result, their teams and the business thrived. Under her guidance, a few corporate relationships were soon formed. Josephine was rewarded for her role and her continued dedication. Within a year, she received a promotion. Josephine was made the VP of Operations.

Josephine's connections in the community were unparalleled, like those within the organization. She had become the name and the face of the organization to clients, stakeholders, and government officials. She seemed to have an innate sense of what they would need and how to satisfy their concerns. And they liked her too. Clients would ask for her by name. Government officials would request her involvement. Her depth of knowledge and reach made Josephine almost godlike to those within the organization. Everyone trusted Josephine.

By the time Josephine finished her third year as the VP of Operations, the organization had boasted close to 300 employees across five divisions and showed signs of continued growth. Huge by comparison, the teams held much the same roles as had existed when the business was first born two decades prior. Layers had been added, processes had been updated or changed, and new services came into being. But essentially, the function and goals of the company remained the same.

As VP of Operations, Josephine's role had been elevated. She was expected to expand the business beyond the current jurisdictional levels while managing the internal workings. She spent several days each week outside of the office in meetings or traveling. She enjoyed that time immensely. It tapped into her drive to grow the business, gave her the freedom to connect with new people, and provided her with some respite from the intensifying responsibilities she was experiencing in the office.

By contrast, on her office days, Josephine found herself frustrated and inundated by staff needs. A literal line of people would form outside her door, waiting for her attention and expertise—most of them waiting with requests for approval, some coming in need of guidance or support. And to Josephine's dismay, more and more often, they started coming to her with complaints. The number of issues Josephine was providing input on was overwhelming her. Short on time and with diminishing patience, Josephine became more decisive and directive with the internal team. Her time was in high demand, so she no longer had the patience to explain her decisions or the rationale behind supporting one initiative or dismissing another.

Josephine's direct reports, all directors, were a mixed bag of skills and competencies. Some were fine with Josephine's managing them in that manner, while others found it dismissive and frustrating. Perhaps not surprisingly, those most comfortable with Josephine's abbreviated style were those who benefited from it. They included members who routinely received her approval (including the Director of Contract Administration, named Jim) and those who were weak in their respective roles, the latter of whom, with Josephine's micromanagement, could appear to shine.

Those least comfortable with it were the independent thinkers who had new ideas. They didn't like Josephine making hasty decisions or discarding their ideas. They wanted an opportunity to vet things more thoroughly. Maya, Director of Field Operations, was of this ilk. A true go-getter, Maya was consistently identifying new strategies to streamline workflow or improve efficiencies. She was seen by many as the strongest leader under Josephine and the future of the organization. But Maya found Josephine's style of decision-making to be shortsighted and dismissive.

It wasn't long before Jim, the director who routinely received Josephine's blessing while others found their requests shot down, became seen by the other directors as the favorite. Jim had been with the organization longer than most of the other directors. He'd been on Josephine's team before she was promoted to VP, and he had been selected as the one to step into her shoes. His team also had the most glamorous role within the agency, interacting with the entertainment agencies who were a part of their customer base.

Jim and Josephine had formed an easy relationship over the years. Jim, the eager student, was happy for Josephine's input and guidance. Josephine was pleased to have a direct report who shared her passion and dedication for supporting the end customer. Having held the same role, Josephine intimately understood the challenges Jim experienced when working with entertainment agencies. They often wanted exceptions made, rules broken. Jim didn't have the authority to approve their requests, but Josephine did. When Jim came with a problem, Josephine listened to him, trusted him, and always had his back.

Due to the intertwined nature of the work, the other directors routinely found this "siding with Jim" form of decision-making to be the crux of the problem. None more so than Maya. A strong leader in her own right, Maya was the director of a team that often found themselves directly impacted by Josephine's actions. When Jim ignored procedure or over-promised to their clients, it nearly always created timing and scheduling challenges for her and her team. They had to make good on those promises.

Maya needed Jim to follow agreed-upon protocols. She'd developed structures around them that ensured all would run smoothly. But instead, Jim seemed to color outside the lines, expecting that Maya and her team would magically make it all come together. It was a constant source of friction between the two. While Maya was frustrated, Jim, who was already seen by many internal leaders as more of a showman than a worker, more a follower than an innovator, felt secure and happy. To Maya, it simply wasn't fair.

Jim and Maya began bringing their disagreements to Josephine with increasing frequency. True to her roots, Josephine always chose to help the organization grow and supported the end consumer. She wasn't choosing Jim, but rather the business. Nevertheless, Maya began to refer to herself and her team as the "redheaded stepchildren." She felt she and her team's needs were too often and too easily brushed aside by Josephine and disregarded by Jim.

Matters were made worse when Jim adopted Josephine's philosophy of always putting the growth of the business first, figuring out how to make that work, second. But unlike Josephine, Jim was never involved in the hard part: figuring out how to make it all work. He had no concept of the impact he was creating, nor did he seem to care. By supporting the clients, Jim only saw that he was supporting growth and receiving accolades from Josephine. He gave little regard to the fact that he was routinely going outside the guidelines for the department he managed. He seemed unconcerned that their standards were developed for a reason, which was to ensure all the other teams had sufficient time to complete their work (the supportive elements of the process).

Jim asked Josephine for permission to work outside the stated guidelines with increasing regularity. It became so routine, the exception to the rule became as common as the rule itself. With standards no longer clear or defined, more and more often, staff found themselves needing to run things by Josephine and needing her approval. As the head of operations and ultimate decision-maker, the team clamored for Josephine's time and attention. It had become a vicious cycle. The more the team needed her, the less time she had to give them.

Josephine's ease in supporting Jim, while not intending to, ultimately undermined Maya and the other directors. Maya became increasingly frustrated and resentful. She became less willing to cooperate with Jim or his team and increasingly insular with her own. The silos that had developed out of the systemic nature of growth were now occurring due to personal frustrations and an unwillingness to engage.

Maya was not alone in her resentment. Other directors felt put-upon by Josephine's decision-making and Jim's cavalier attitude toward following protocol. Even the remaining two members of the original five were feeling perturbed. Yet Josephine, writing the tensions off as interpersonal disputes, was fixated on the fevered pitch of the work. She began to lean more heavily on the legacy directors who began their tenure beside her so many years before. She trusted they understood the need and would be capable and driven to support the organization. She asked them to provide backup support to Jim's group.

The legacy members did as Josephine asked, but that didn't remove their frustrations. While they recognized the value in supporting the client base, they also noticed a complete lack of reciprocity from Jim and his team. Roles were necessarily intertwined. But focusing on the needs of only one team was causing conflict.

The two legacy directors provided support just as Josephine asked. When Jim's team needed support, they put all hands on deck. But when the workload shifted and the tables turned, they found there was never a time that Jim considered helping them or the other teams in kind. Even as they pointed it out, Jim was dismissive of their requests, saying he needed to preserve his team's availability should a need arise; or that he wanted to give them a much-deserved break during the slower times. These legacy directors, senior members of the organization, were supporting younger, newer, less skilled members of the team and with remarkably low appreciation. It was becoming intolerable.

What had been the recipe for success in those early days was lost but not simply due to growth. The magic was gone because support and resources were constantly flowing in the same direction instead of moving around fluidly between the groups as they had back in the early days. Increasingly, for those two legacy directors, it felt less like they were supporting the organization and more like they were supporting an unappreciative member of the team: Jim.

As head of operations, Josephine was ostensibly leading all these teams. However, she took only fleeting notice of the issues. Bogged down with client-oriented requests, she kept her focus on the needs immediately before her. And with a line out the door, this meant little if any of her attention was geared toward attending to team member discord.

Josephine had become myopic. She didn't see the bigger issues. She wasn't managing the brewing conflict among her team leaders.

Despite her growing discontent, Maya stopped bringing her concerns to Josephine. Unlike Jim, her needs were rarely met that way. She understood Josephine's leanings and limited time for managing the team. She would figure it out on her own.

Maya was determined to protect her team and defend her efforts at providing stability for the organization. She had worked hard to bring efficiencies and improvements. But all of that was falling by the wayside. Things were increasingly askew. Her team was continually impacted, often working overtime or changing plans, and twice even canceling a vacation to accommodate the needs of the business.

For Maya, it was all too much. To address her team's needs, she would need to do something. She started by adding a layer of bureaucracy, effectively slowing down Jim's ability to create new requests. She then limited her interactions with Jim, ensuring he couldn't sidle up to her with requests when she wasn't prepared to say no. Finally, when they did speak, Maya was unyielding to Jim's requests. Her goal was to protect her team and reignite the protocols that kept things running smoothly. Either her efforts would work, and things would shift back into place, or she would force a wake-up call for both Jim and Josephine. She was looking forward to the change either way.

However, Maya's team was not thrilled with this turn of events. They liked and trusted Maya. They knew her resistance was being taken in their defense. Yet her actions also put them in a challenging position. Maya's team held a largely supportive role to Jim's team, while Jim's team directly connected to the clients. Not only did Jim's team have the more glamorous role, connecting with entertainment industry clients, with Josephine's support, it also meant his team had more opportunities for acknowledgment and advancement in the organization. If they had any hopes of moving into the client-oriented side of the business or receiving a promotion, following their leader, Maya, would compromise their future. Those who had imagined a future within the organization became concerned that they had no avenue for success. A few key members of Maya's team quit. The loss of staff further compromised the already tense situation.

Jim had become aware of an issue soon after Maya dug her heels in the sand. She refused to reschedule her team to accommodate his. She wouldn't authorize their overtime when he needed them to work long hours. She, in part, blamed it on staffing. But she also remarked offhandedly to Jim that it was only necessary because he was skirting protocol. She reminded him that he should let his team and the clients know of scheduling limitations.

Jim angrily went to Josephine for guidance and support. And, expectedly, Josephine called Maya into that meeting.

While Josephine listened to both team members, ultimately, she gave Maya the dressing down, directing her to change her antics and to support Jim's team. Maya was fed up. She went to the company's Human Resources department.

Maya's complaints about favoritism and an unhealthy work culture were not new to the HR team. While she had more pointed examples, the HR team had heard complaints from others as they cited Josephine's struggles with leadership. They knew of the lines that formed outside her door. They were aware that protocols were not being followed and that overtime, and the budgetary issues it presented, were the result. They had long before been concerned about Josephine's fitness as a leader. But the HR team was also in a tough spot. Josephine was the heart and blood of the organization. She was the face to their stakeholders and the keeper of all institutional knowledge. Josephine was considered untouchable.

FINDING THE GAP — THE LEADER'S ABYSS

Finding the problems and identifying what will fix them is rarely self-evident to a leader. If it were easy to locate or simple to fix, most leaders would get it done. But it often takes an outside influence.

Once the HR team at Josephine's company became involved, the stakes for everyone were higher. While the HR leader recognized that many of the issues stemmed from Josephine's leadership, she too was unclear on what specific changes were needed. She was also acutely aware that Josephine's deep roots in the company, including relationships with government officials, key stakeholders, and top clients—meant managing her would be next to impossible. As the Chief Operating Officer, Josephine managed nearly their entire workforce, directly or indirectly. And she exhibited strong resistance to feedback, at least from those who lacked her historical knowledge of the organization. The HR team was at a loss.

The issues Josephine was causing tore at the very fabric of what made the business function: teamwork. There were tensions among the teams. Frustrations and complaints were occurring with increasing frequency and intensity. Less-competent team members were promoted while others who demonstrated promise—those taking on greater responsibility and accountability—were held back. Decision-making had become largely one-sided, and workflow was disproportionately impacting certain teams.

The HR team brought me in to unravel the conflict. By interviewing Josephine and her team, I became privy to their issues and began to see what needed to change, particularly from their leader. Josephine was exhausted and irritated. She knew she had become short and direct with the team but saw no alternative. She failed to fulfill her leadership role of expanding the business, yet managing the team didn't afford her the time to do much else.

Josephine did not, however, notice that her lack of role clarity was responsible for her team's dependence on her. She didn't recognize her actions were feeding the problem and causing her to feel deeply frustrated and overwhelmed. She genuinely wanted things to be different, but she didn't know what to change.

Josephine's shortcomings were a byproduct of her passion and unending commitment to the organization's future. She cared for the business as one might a child. And, just as some parents have a hard time stepping back and letting go, so was true of Josephine. Her leadership issues came not from self-aggrandizing or self-importance but love. She cared so deeply about the business's success, she couldn't let go.

Josephine's leadership was impacted by issues of

- Trust
- Role Clarity
- Conflict Management

While each of these is significant on its own, for Josephine, they transpired in concert with one another, each impacting the other. The resulting cacophony led to issues with accountability, stifled growth, and loss of talent. Just as was true of our other leaders, Josephine was not awakened to her full role as a leader. She was unaware that she was creating many of her own struggles. Josephine's actions had been made with a blind focus on supporting the organization. But her best intentions were certainly not being realized.

TRUST

Trust was Josephine's most fundamental struggle. Her focus remained rooted in the past—back when the rules were being formed and still flexible.

She didn't believe their clients would accept a more formal and consistent process. She didn't embrace that the organization's importance, position, and value had become readily identifiable to anyone. She didn't trust that her team and the company would be able to flourish without her direct and constant oversight.

As a result, her fear of the business's potential demise overruled her actions and decision-making. Her deep care and concern for an organization that had grown so strong were still causing her to stay involved in places where, in her role, she no longer belonged. While Josephine considered her direct oversight of the team to be essential for keeping her aware of potential problems, she didn't see that it also left her mired in the role of a staff member. Rather than trust her team, she continued to shepherd the business the ways she always had.

Josephine's strategies weren't preventing any problems or helping foster growth as she had intended. They created a self-fulfilling prophecy where clients expected the rules to be bent in their favor. They were sheltering her team from learning and decision-making, keeping them dependent upon her. Her trust issues left her responsible for everything. She was utterly overtaxed and overwhelmed, and still, the problems were spiraling out of control.

ROLE CLARITY

As a legacy leader, Josephine found it challenging to manage the shift in roles. She took pride in having had a fundamental role in building the business. By being part of the organization's foundation, helping it to grow and thrive, and seeing the fruits of her labor, Josephine developed an indelible connection to the business and its success.

Revisiting the analogy of Josephine's attachment to the work, the business was like her baby. Though now "grown-up," Josephine struggled to let it go. She struggled to change her role to mirror its growth and emerging needs.

All parents experience this as their child grows and seeks independence. The frequent arguments, particularly during adolescence, are built out of a child's desire to develop independence, coupled with their parents' need to provide guidance and support. Even young adults going to college, starting careers, getting married, and starting families of their own have parents still apt to step in, advise, and lead their children in the direction they believe best. It's hard to develop trust and change our roles—to move from guardian and caretaker to advisor and observer.

The difference between the child and the business is that the child, cum adult, is a sentient being, one who will fight to break free and become independent from their parent. An adolescent will take action and force a new relationship to develop. A business puts up no such fight. It shows no obvious distress at being guided, managed, and structured. For this reason, even as she moved up in ranks, Josephine found it incredibly hard to let go of her earlier role in building the business.

Beyond the challenge of letting go was that Josephine's advancement, like most legacy leaders, was incremental. She never let go of one rung before grabbing hold of the next. Initially, it seemed essential. Her small but growing team would look to her for advice and wisdom. She enjoyed guiding the work and supporting the business and team. She didn't recognize that she was micromanaging them. She didn't foresee that it would evolve into dependency. But as the team's reliance continued and her responsibilities increased, Josephine had to double her efforts to keep up with the demands on her time. She became hyper-responsible and, as a result, completely overwhelmed. She was managing her new role while still maintaining a hold on the roles of others.

Adding to the challenge, some team members embraced her oversight and guidance. Jim benefited greatly by staying tightly aligned with Josephine. He was credited for his team's successes while being sheltered from responsibility. Other staff similarly benefited from this, especially those who lacked competency but appeared capable under Josephine's tutelage. Her strong oversight meant she was doing the job and taking the responsibility of several members of her team. Her micromanagement undermined team accountability while leaving her stretched thin.

Finally, Josephine's challenges with role clarity included her over-involvement in decision-making. Because of her high level within the organization, her habit of changing the rules rather than following protocol wasn't challenged by anyone.

Nevertheless, those behaviors led to a line out her door, giving her feelings of overwhelm while simultaneously diminishing the ability of her direct-report managers to demonstrate accountability for their roles.

CONFLICT MANAGEMENT

A leader with healthy role clarity is not typically drawn into team-level conflict. Yet Josephine often found herself in the middle of it, unclear of her role, and unable to manage the conflicts her team brought to her door. Her propensity to make exceptions and ignore protocol left her over-involved in decision-making. The seemingly inconsequential action of helping set priorities and determine exceptions to policy (which had once been a part of her role) kept her engaged in what should have become routine decisions for her team to make. Josephine's trust and role clarity issues created a domino effect, leading to internal conflicts.

While Josephine held the role of their leader, she was participating at the same level as her team. She continued to make decisions as she had when she was responsible for Contract Administration. Despite her good intentions, this pattern created the kernel for conflict, Jim and his team routinely benefiting from her decisions, while the other groups found themselves adversely affected. By assuming this dual role of leader and team member, Josephine caused the staff to sense favoritism.

Beyond the discontent that ensued, Josephine inevitably became the arbiter of every disagreement or dispute, especially those brought about by her own involvement. When her decisions caused friction, she was still the one to settle the differences. It became akin to a parent/child dynamic, where the kids argue and expect the parent will decide who is right. Except Josephine seemed to always be on the side of the same child.

Josephine lacked the time and inclination to engage her team fully in these discussions. She was already overwhelmed by maintaining the various aspects of her role (including those aspects she no longer should have held), and the conflicts, to her, were unnecessary. Her interest wasn't in taking sides but expediency. Her intention was not to create favoritism but to protect the business. Rather than get into the weeds, Josephine dismissed the conflict by taking ownership of having made the decision, expecting the team to move on.

The problem with managing conflict in that manner, as Josephine soon found, is that it quickly creates a feeling of inequality. Fairness concerns, claims of favoritism, discontent, and loss of talent all grow out of this pattern of conflict management. Josephine wasn't managing conflict. She was trying to eliminate it. She was metaphorically telling it and her team to "go away."

Because of that, some directors, Maya in particular, took matters into their own hands. The aftermath led to a divided team, unwanted turnover, and damage to the reputation and motivation of a rising star: Maya.

WHAT I FOUND

When I first came to work with Josephine and her team, the group seemed relatively stable. They appeared to engage easily with one another. There were no obvious signs of resistance or tension. But meetings with the individuals told a different story. While the team members shared a genuine like and affection for one another, their professional issues were brimming with intensity.

The negative energy was largely aimed at Jim and Josephine. While the directors' grievances concentrated primarily on Jim's behavior—his sense of entitlement, his failures to reciprocate, his attitude of superiority—it wasn't without a shared focus on Josephine's leadership: her allowing it to happen and her unwavering support of their wayward team member.

Josephine was struggling as a leader because she was unaware of her role and the impact it created. She was overwhelmed yet afraid to trust her team and let go of her prior responsibilities. She was determined to inspire collaboration and teamwork. Yet, she directed her team to pitch in, thereby undermining any hope for the magic and camaraderie she had felt in those early days of the once fledgling business. For all her good intentions, Josephine's efforts were doing more harm than good.

Josephine was stuck in a pattern that was generating problems for the team not solving them. The lack of trust and muddied roles were creating friction and dissonance. Josephine led with her heart, her love for the business, and her desire to instill great teamwork. But her efforts were falling far short of her ideals. Like many leaders, she was blind to the error of her ways. Josephine did not know what she did not know. Her problems were rooted in the gap.

PART THREE

FIX

INTRODUCTION TO FIX

To overcome our challenges,
all that is required is the courage to ask for help.

—Simon Sinek

Do you like to learn your lessons the hard way—by experiencing the pain of every misstep and decision firsthand? I bet not. Intelligent people prefer to learn from others. Why else would you read business books, attend conferences, and engage in learning? To build on what is already available.

Where FIND was your storyteller, FIX is your teacher. FIX is designed to build on the stories and teach you the lessons within. The lessons are deep and layered, full of insight, and steeped in information that drives emotional intelligence. FIX breathes new awareness into your life.

In FIX, I carry forward the stories already shared and invest more fully into the changes needed. I also broaden the scope of the stories to expose other problems leaders experience related to issues with trust, role clarity, and conflict management.

As you read FIX, you will begin to know which changes will be most important or meaningful for you and your company. In turn, you will find the steps toward change come more easily, more naturally, and become much more lasting.

What else can you expect?

No doubt, you have read other business books and received helpful guidance on things *to do*. This section goes a step further. FIX provides you with guidance on what *not* to do. Beyond a red-flag warning, in FIX, I will expose the ramifications you can expect if you still choose to move forward with a "don't do it" action. Knowing what not to do is often invaluable information. It can save you from damaging your relationships, being blindsided by conflict, inflaming the issues, and creating a whole host of related problems.

I am reminded of a friendly meeting I had several years back with two employment attorneys. These attorneys, both respected leaders in their field, often referred clients to me. One day, they had invited me to lunch to bend my ear. As we ate our salads, they shared details of some drama in their office. Initially, they were focused on telling me their story and invited my opinion on how to handle the situation. But very quickly, as they dug in on what was happening, they began to riff more with one another, identifying what they thought they needed to do and how they would address things.

As they strategized with one another, I started hearing red flags and tried to intervene. It was clear to me that the ideas they were dreaming up would inflame the drama and shame the employee. But in their animated discussion, they had stopped paying attention to me.

I finally interrupted. "Can you not hear how loudly I am shaking my head?"

They stopped, bewildered.

I then asked them what the intent of their strategy was—to shame their team member or get her on the right track?

Conversations like these are not atypical. I have had similar conversations with many business owners and leaders. They use me as a sounding board, especially for the difficult conversations they need to hold. Our conversations invariably include guidance on what not to do or say in their situation and the reasons behind it.

For the attorneys I was lunching with, it was only after I explained what was wrong with their plan that they could embrace what might be right with another plan. I have found that is true for most people but especially for those who are educated and accomplished—leaders like you.

As you read FIX, you will learn how to fix the leadership issues impacting you, your team, and your business. You will begin the journey toward closing the gap.

CHAPTER SIX

TRUST

We never get the opportunity to be successful if we never confront the opportunity to fail.

As entrepreneurs or legacy leaders, we don't trust, because there is so much to lose. We feel we can't afford to let someone make a mistake. It's like a parent that doesn't want their child to fall. But a child that never falls never learns how to pick themselves up again. Management fails when we don't permit the business (team) to fall. When we think the fall will be so cataclysmic that we cannot recover. And that's almost never the truth. We need to recognize it's not cataclysmic, and to let the mistake happen. To let it be a teaching moment.

Tony Rose, *Founding Partner Rose, Snyder, and Jacobs, LLP*

Trust comes from a belief that we can rely on the integrity, strength, or surety of something. Without trust, we would never step foot on an airplane or a boat; a mountain climber would never experience the freedom of repelling down a cliff; and the concept of space travel would be limited to our imaginations. Each of these advances in our human experience is only possible because it's been proven that they are safe. However, these are all objects of the physical world where we can measure safety and improve upon it—where we can calculate lift, buoyancy, trajectory, and weight capacity—where we stress-test reactions and quadruple-check every factor. In the physical world, we can guarantee safety, and therefore others can begin to trust.

When it comes to trust in our relationships, this is far different. Trust in another person, whether social, marital, or work-related, is not straightforward. It is not based on mathematical calculations, scientific evidence, or quantifiable proof. Instead, relational trust is a byproduct of experience, faith, and sometimes, hope. Rather than proven, relational trust is cemented in our *confidence* in another person.

Your confidence to go under the knife of a surgeon is no doubt based upon the reputation and experience of the physician. You consider relative risk versus reward for undergoing the procedure. Your willingness to eat in a restaurant or attend a neighborhood potluck is based on your knowledge of who prepared the food and your faith that it was prepared in a sanitary environment. Here again, a sense of safety begets trust.

In a business setting, trust develops differently still. While akin to our social world, we find that in our working relationships, safety is less guaranteed. The ability to identify reputation proves both challenging and unreliable. In a workplace setting, the motivations behind a person's actions and behaviors can be opaque, scrutinized, and questioned.

Often, staff initiates their work together, having no history to draw upon. Their ability to team or collaborate comes primarily from each person's sense of responsibility to perform well and the essential interconnection of their job duties. Trust is not the stabilizing force behind their collaboration, only self-interest, self-preservation. They want to keep their job. A staff member's trust in their leader begins in the same way.

Trust Takes Time

The surgeon. The pilot. The daycare provider. Would you be comfortable putting your life or the life of someone you love in the hands of a surgeon, a pilot, or a daycare provider if you had no way of verifying their reputation or experience? Of course not. There are licenses, standards, and regulatory agencies for that exact purpose: to create a sense of trust when we must engage with a stranger.

To fully trust in another, we must first feel safe. To feel safe, we must have confidence in our ability to predict the other person's behavior. Online reviews and regulatory data do not exist on a person-to-person level. For that reason, particularly in a workplace setting, trust takes time. It is a derivative of predictability and a reflection of demonstrated dependability, which, when combined, allows us to feel safe. Trust, therefore, cannot be given. It must be earned over time.

When we willingly place our trust in someone, it is because we have seen a steady and consistent pattern of positive behavior from them. That pattern yields our sense of safety and, therefore, our trust. Your employees are no different. Their sense of safety, and therefore trust in you as their leader, is the byproduct of your predictability in three key areas:

- Your ability (work performance)
- Your positive intentions
- Your genuine care or concern for them

The first is the simplest. It is presumed that you are in your position because you have the capacity and knowledge to perform well. Your team trusts in your ability to reach goals, make good choices, and help the company succeed. The other two qualities essential for demonstrating your trustworthiness, however, are not so quickly bestowed.

Establishing your positive intent takes time. There's no shortcut. It is the byproduct of multiple interactions and inescapably comes from how each team member assesses you in those situations. As each person sees the decisions and choices you make, they will discern who you are and what you care about through *their* lens. It's not a conscious action. Yet, it informs them of how well your intentions and priorities align with their own. What do you care about? Are you ethical? Are you in it for yourself or the company? Regardless of whether their assessment of you is accurate, their read on your intentions is silently recorded in their impression of you and has a bearing on the relationship (and trust) you cultivate.

Finally, to develop trust in you, each member of your team must believe you care about them and will protect them. This is not something you can fake. An employee will not feel cared for just because you greet them warmly, celebrate their birthday, or have a habit of saying please and thank you. Indeed, those are appreciated, but they are superficial. Your team will feel cared for when they believe you respect and value them *professionally*. They will recognize that you are interested in them when you ask for their opinion, acknowledge their strengths, give credit for their contribution to an idea, and support their growth.

Because trust is built on predictability, its development is incremental. Some staff will develop trust in you more quickly than others. Some will need more time, more experience, or more proof that your intentions are pure. Certainly, each team member comes to the table with their own experiences. These color their ability and timeline for developing trust in you. Your consistency in demonstrating that you value them and that your intentions are positive are your keys to gaining their trust.

We'll now dive deeper and explore the role trust played in each of our stories. Since Gary's struggles are most notably connected with creating *foundational* trust, we'll start with him.

GARY'S ASSUMPTIONS – "TRUST ME"

Gary embraced his new leadership role at the university with a presumption that the faculty would trust him. Having no history or baggage with anyone in the department, he expected they would see him as objective, having a clean slate, and therefore immediately trustworthy. Gary saw himself that way. He was the voice of reason, helpful, and unbiased. Gary was the self-described "benevolent dictator." With his presumptions of being immediately trustworthy firmly in place, Gary made decisions and changes without engaging much with others. He believed it was a wise approach. There would be no appearance of impropriety, and it would ensure those with ulterior motives didn't sway him. He created an open-door policy to balance his decisions and create an opportunity for the team to feel heard. Finally, to secure the faculty's trust, he promised confidentiality to those who came to him with a concern or complaint.

It might seem Gary was worthy of his staff's trust. He gave them a safe space to talk. He made changes that reflected their concerns. He protected them from attack or retribution by keeping their conversations confidential.

Essentially, the staff *did* trust him. But Gary's actions for developing trust were grossly misguided. He made changes without exploring the impact. He used "trust me" in place of an explanation. The inevitable result not only undermined the faculty's trust in him, but more concerningly, led to rumors, fear, silos, and divisiveness among dozens of faculty members.

There are many lessons we can learn from Gary.

"Trust Me" Isn't Enough

As a leader, you sometimes lack time to allow trust to grow organically. For expediency, you may say, as Gary often did, "Trust me" to members of your team. How often might you have said those exact words? Under what circumstances might you still say them? Saying, "Trust me" is deeply consequential. Here's why.

First, while you've likely never given it much thought, when a person says, "Trust me," it is because they are withholding information. Sure, it is a common colloquialism, but the expression is the equivalent of saying, "I need you to follow my lead," or "I need you to have my back on this," while it simultaneously implies, "Don't ask me any questions." For that reason, in a business setting, the expression causes others to ponder, *What are you hiding?* Or *who are you trying to protect?* Saying, "Trust me" without further explanation does not instill confidence or promote a sense of safety. It engenders suspicion. That was the case for Gary and his team.

Second, when a member of your team hears you say, "Trust me," they will infer that you know something they do not, and more to the point, that you are not sharing the information you possess. While it may be factually accurate, as the leader you *are* privy to more information; it nevertheless will cause them to speculate. Why can't you share rather than ask for the benefit of the doubt? (After all, that expression alone highlights the point, there is reason to doubt). Denying your team clarifying information only exacerbates that sentiment. They are left to wonder why you don't trust *them* and willingly provide them with all the information at hand?

That occurred when Gary dismissed the gossip and rumors forming among his faculty and when, rather than provide clarity or transparency, he remained silent then implored his faculty to trust him.

Third, and most concerningly, the phrase "Trust me" can be used to ask someone to ignore something they know, saw, or overheard. Here, the expression asks a person to set aside their own judgment and ignore their instincts. In this way, the expression "Trust me" asks one to trust whoever is making the request more than they trust their own perceptions. Gary's actions tiptoed into this territory when he refused to discuss or provide clarity about circumstances to which others had become privy. Instead of giving information, he again defaulted to "Trust me."

Gary's frequent requests to trust him directly undermined any sense of psychological safety within the department. The term, psychological safety, was first coined by Dr. Amy Edmonson, a professor at Harvard Business School. It is used to describe team dynamics and refers to "a shared belief that the team is safe for interpersonal risk-taking." Psychological safety has since been referenced by countless organizations as an identifier for the strength of their teams.

In 2015, industry giant Google embarked on a deep internal study on teamwork. Their researchers found that the number-one driver of high-performing teams was a feeling of team psychological safety.

Google researchers further determined "who is on the team matters less than how the team members interact, structure their work, and view their contributions."

McKinsey & Company, a global management consulting firm who are trusted advisors to the world's leading businesses, governments, and institutions notes, "A leader, sets the tone for the team climate through their own actions. Team leaders have the strongest influence on a team's psychological safety." (De Smet, Rubenstein, Vierow, 2021)

Gary's team, through his frequent use of "Trust me" in lieu of sharing information, learned that their work environment was not safe.

The request for trust cannot take the place of building a trusting relationship or be used as a substitute for offering an explanation. To do so only serves to exploit the very quality of trust one hopes to achieve.

Building and Maintaining a Trust Account

Rather than asking for a person's blind trust, which breeds insecurity, you must build a stable structure of trust with your team.

To illustrate the concept of building trust, let's imagine a bank account. Say you open a new bank account and deposit a small sum of money to establish that account. The bank, happy to have this new relationship, will undoubtedly allow you to withdraw money at your leisure but limit you to the money you have deposited. In a workplace setting, an equivalently small step toward developing trust would be accomplished through being present and involved and saying hello to your team.

Now, let's say you were to ask your bank for a loan or make a withdrawal that exceeds what you have in your account. The bank would either decline or ask for significantly more verification of your worthiness to borrow these funds. Even when you and the bank have established a long relationship and there are significant funds in your account, borrowing beyond the deposited funds will still require disclosure of information. The same holds with building trust from your team.

As you make significant "deposits," by sharing information, being open and honest, asking for others' input or opinions, etc., you build equity in the trust of your people. Over time, small deposits into your trust account will allow it to grow. A small withdrawal from the trust account, perhaps by neglecting to inform a team member of some noncritical details, will hardly be noticed.

You will find your store of trust becomes incredibly stable. You notice your team comfortably follows your guidance or supports new initiatives without much question. They demonstrate loyalty and show complete faith in your leadership. Still, even at that point of high stability, large transactions will require an explanation.

Spending your Trust Account

When you have built trust with your team over time, you can make changes and ask things of them that require their trust. However, it is essential that you do not overestimate how much trust they have in you.

Imagine, for instance, that you have remained silent about an upcoming merger or layoff that your team has become aware of. With a large trust account, this situation, while concerning and unpleasant, will be more readily accepted. On the contrary, for the leader without an established trust account, it can be disastrous. But beware, even with a well-funded trust account, large withdrawals of this kind still need to be repaid in the form of an explanation about the silence. Your team will want to understand why they were not informed. They will want to ask questions, and they will expect legitimate answers.

A leader who hedges when answering those kinds of questions or gives incomplete information will never rise above this questioning. Their reluctance to share will build doubt in their team, depleting the trust account. Both Stuart (our leader who built his team with a focus on friendship) and Gary (our benevolent dictator) suffered this. Each damaged the trust of their team by neglecting to share information or include their team in the discussion.

Taking this concept one step further, let's consider the parallel between trust built from your team and trust built in a marital relationship. You engage in each of these relationships with long-term expectations. You know you will be spending significant time together. And in both, you recognize that your decisions and actions have an impact on the other party. Finally, in both relationships, there is an expectation of trust and respect.

Keeping with this parallel, let's continue to examine our banking analogy for developing trust. Imagine your spouse adds or removes a small amount of funds from your joint account. There is probably no need for concern or discussion. You trust your spouse. You accept that many decisions are made without your involvement. However, imagine that a major transaction suddenly appeared—something unexpected and out of the ordinary. You would undoubtedly expect a conversation with your spouse to explain it. Absent such communication, or worse, their refusal to engage in a discussion about the transaction, and you are likely to be concerned. A "trust me" response given in place of full details would likely add to your concern. Why? You love your spouse. You trust them. Why do you need an explanation?

We react with concern because being told, "Trust me" suggests that some part of the information behind the decision might not be acceptable or agreed upon. It speaks to secrecy.

Trust is fragile, and secrecy is its biggest enemy.

A business relationship is no different. If anything, it is even more fragile. The secrecy from a leader often causes even more speculation and concern.

Transparency

Transparency, or lack thereof, is directly related to trust. As Gary and Stuart both found, a failure to provide transparency will cost you trust. The damage will occur whether employees figure things out on their own or are suddenly but belatedly informed of changes that have been orchestrated behind the scenes. The more successful a leader is at concealing information, the more they have accomplished blindsiding their employees and creating an environment rife with rumor and speculation.

Even if a situation seems benign to you, a lack of transparency can make it seem massive to your team. I came across a simple example of this during a recent and routine visit to my allergist.

As I arrived at the office, I immediately noticed half the office space was closed off. There were signs posted indicating it was temporary. I wondered about it; perhaps they were doing a remodel?

The other patients and I were minorly inconvenienced as we were routed around the facility to bypass the front office, which was under construction. Once meeting with the nurse, I asked if she was excited about the office remodel.

Her face contorted slightly. "I guess," she said.

Noticing her displeasure, I acknowledged that change is hard. Then, trying to build a bit of optimism, I asked her about the future look and function of the space.

Rather than build positivity, the nurse gloomily informed me that she had no idea what it would look like. She only just found out. It seems she and the rest of the staff were told only the day before the remodel. She shared that she and the rest of the staff were informed because they needed to remove patient files and front-office supplies to another location. She did not know the plan in advance, nor any information about the reason behind it. She didn't know how long the process would take or what would be different after the remodel.

I acknowledged the stress this must have caused and reflected that she must be experiencing some trust issues.

She looked me square in the eyes and said, "Exactly."

That nurse, a long-term trusted member of the team, was utterly blindsided about the changes now underway in her office. She felt betrayed by the secrecy around the decision. The message it sent was solid and negative: the staff has very little value to those in charge of decision-making. It left the nurse, and probably the rest of the team, wondering; if they couldn't be forthcoming with something as innocuous as an office redesign, what else are they withholding? What's next? Are our jobs safe?

Even if a change seems innocuous, such as the redesign of an office space, leaders will find their actions have come at a cost to the team's willingness or ability to trust, have buy-in, or support the change. They have made a substantial sacrifice in the name of expediency.

Instead, when there is transparency, employees are unlikely to question their job security or doubt if the company is working honorably to care for them financially. They feel a significant degree of security by knowing the truth behind decisions and seeing where things are headed on their team or within the company.

Being transparent with your team where and whenever possible is critical. It builds trust. It brings peace of mind. And when there is an occasion where it needs to be handled differently, there is a bank account of trust that has been accruing interest and gives the employees something to hold onto while they await clarity and information.

STUART'S MISGUIDED EFFORTS TO BUILD TRUST

Stuart, honored to be building a new team of directors, quickly built a moderate level of trust with his team, one that was built on a shared vision of success. Stuart had painted a picture of what his group could achieve, and the team was committed to doing so. Everyone thought they were on the same page.

However, that promise seemed broken and the vision of success crushed when problems Stuart had agreed to resolve, such as those with Oliver, remained unchanged despite mounting evidence about the damage they were causing. Stuart's seemingly blasé attitude about the problem inflamed tensions further. The team relied on Stuart for creating fluidity and collaboration. Their trust was built largely on his ability to establish and maintain their collective responsibility so they could be successful. Feeling a frightening lack of support and sensing no alternative, the team decided to address the issues themselves. However, as Stuart learned of this, he condemned the team for their actions. He added insult to injury.

Trust is Earned, Not Bestowed

When people have to manage the dangers from inside the organization, the organization itself becomes less able to face the dangers from outside.

—Simon Sinek

Stuart expected the team to trust him even as his actions supported their problem-causing colleague. The analogy of a bank account is fitting. Beyond Stuart's word, the team had no evidence that he was acting on their behalf. Therefore, the lack of change in Oliver's behavior required the team to invest in increasing levels of trust to believe that Stuart was indeed representing them. Finally, when the team challenged Stuart about this, his default response was to say, "Trust me," a request we already know to be deeply flawed. Stuart had not maintained his account, yet he continued to draw down on its fund until he was deeply in the negative.

In a professional relationship, and particularly from a leader, trust should never be used as a statement reflecting, "Either you believe me, or you don't." That was the essence of Stuart's reaction and mindset. Such a response doesn't solve the problem, nor does it build confidence that things will improve.

Best-Selling author, Nan Russell, in her book the *The Titleless Leader* explains, "Trust begins with trust. You don't get trust because you earn it; you get it because you give it. Trust is a verb. It's an action. Giving trust is a choice or judgment you make when you put confidence in or rely on someone else."

Un-learning Some Not-So-Sage Advice

Stuart had faced a conundrum—how to assure his team of the efforts he was making while still respecting the privacy of the individual? He was following the sage though imperfect advice to "Praise publicly and criticize privately."

The problem with following this adage is that sometimes when you hold a corrective conversation privately, it doesn't lead to change. Worse still, unless you are directly impacted by the actions of that person, you may not be aware that the issues are persisting. Meanwhile, a lot can be happening in the background.

For example, still experiencing the problems, the team may doubt that you have engaged the problem person or that any conversation about change has genuinely occurred. In that case, the team is left to wonder, do you genuinely respect them and their concerns, or are you merely giving lip service to their complaints?

It is also possible that the person receiving your feedback (Oliver in Stuart's case) may not fully trust the validity of the information you have shared. Your Oliver may even believe he is being singled out or picked on by you or his colleagues.

In addition, without an opportunity to ask questions, gain clarity, or offer an explanation, what you have shared has left your problem team member in a compromised position. Unable to have a conversation or explain, and unable to fully grasp their impact on the team, how can your problem person appropriately change?

Finally, keep this in mind: when issues continue to surface, it isn't necessarily the fault of the problem team member. It may be that you have not adequately identified the problem, the team member disagreed that they were the cause of the problem, or perhaps they didn't like your proposed solution. In any event, to criticize privately when you are not likely to witness or experience the desired change leaves all aspects of the interaction up for speculation. While you may still choose to follow this pattern, it is essential to understand that when an issue is *not* successfully resolved through private conversation, a team conversation will be necessary.

In Chapter 13, Critical Conversations, I break down the factors for determining when a corrective conversation should be held privately and when it is necessary to do so in a group setting. For now, I want to offer you three strategies that support maintaining trust with your team while simultaneously circumventing the challenges inherent in managing issues privately.

Strategies to Support Trust

First, adjust your mindset when considering a problem. The tendency toward blame is strong; to manage it, alter the lens through which you view the problem and the people. Vindicate; don't villainize. This is important not only for you, but through your communication about the issue, you will also be modeling and instilling that mindset on your team.

Adopt the position that the problem person has good reasons for their behavior. Similarly, trust that the team is well-meaning and purposeful in their desire to bring about change. By vindicating, you accept that the problem person is unaware of the negative impact they are having. Or, as in Oliver's case, they are naïve and therefore cannot recognize that the problems they create outweigh any positive results.

You refrain from blame by embracing a standpoint to vindicate not villainize. As a result, defenses stay low, and listening and understanding improve.

Second, enhance your communication. When tensions arise among your team, distrust is already an underlying component. Your role in helping, rather than adding to the chaos, will require you to keep the doors of communication wide open.

Keep your team informed of your efforts. Proactively share that you have spoken with the individual creating concerns (Oliver in our example) and offer the group an update based on your efforts. Likewise, communicate openly with "Oliver," informing him of your plan to keep the team in the loop about both your discussion and of his (Oliver's) commitment to bringing about change.

Third, stay involved. Ensure all team members know that you want to be kept informed of any improvement or lack thereof so that you can keep in front of the problem. That level of transparency allows you to hold the meeting privately while keeping the team informed of your efforts to bring substantive change. Asking the group to report back, ostensibly providing support if they advise you that your recent efforts have not been successful, demonstrates your commitment to addressing the problem fully.

If this effort at communication seems gossipy to you, it is because you have not yet adopted an understanding of transparency. While it is not appropriate to share the full details of the corrective conversation, it is reasonable to share the key points. For example, Stuart could have said to the team, "This morning, I spoke to Oliver about the issues you have described to me. He committed that he would make an effort to change, and I suggested he connect with you individually if he would like more specific details. Should you find Oliver is not changing his behavior, please gently point that out to him, but also, let me know so that I may stay on top of this."

In the example above, Stuart followed all three strategies to support trust when speaking with his team:

"This morning, I spoke with Oliver about the issues you have described to me. He committed to making an effort to change, and I suggested he connect with you individually if he would like more specific details [Enhanced Communication]. Should you find Oliver is not changing his behavior, please gently point that out to him [Mindset of Vindicate Not Villainize], but also, let me know so that I may stay on top of this" [Stay Involved].

When you recognize that trust is earned and not bestowed, it becomes clear that trust requires an ongoing effort. Communicating openly and staying involved builds a platform of transparency that builds trust not only with you but among your team. Similarly, trust is enhanced by adopting the philosophy to vindicate, not villainize, when you attend to an issue. The efforts you make will be noticed by your team and are likely to be mirrored back in return. Trust is reciprocal.

JOSEPHINE'S RELIANCE ON CONTROL OVER TRUST

Josephine's issues with trust were far different from those of Stuart or Gary. She had been at her company from its beginning and was instrumental in its growth and success. She was knowledgeable, caring, and dedicated. Her team trusted in her ability, they trusted in her intentions, they trusted that she cared about the business. The problem was, Josephine didn't trust her team in return.

As a legacy leader whose direct involvement had been indispensable in the early years, Josephine was unable to accept that the business could survive without her direct oversight. Rather than trust her team, she stayed involved. Rather than accept mistakes as normal, perhaps even necessary for growth, she intervened, attempting to prevent them.

Josephine's struggles with trust were evident in her micromanagement and over-involvement.

Perhaps understandably, Josephine's focus remained as it always had been: protecting the business. For her, it meant service to the clients and keeping them happy. The result, however, meant her staying involved on a far too granular level, effectively usurping the authority of her team while caving into requests that should have been denied.

Ideally, Josephine would have seen the strength of the business and mirrored that strength back to the clients. She would have openly and matter-of-factly informed them of emerging changes in process and procedure. She would have recognized that boundaries are healthy and necessary for growth, and she would have supported her team in taking charge, even if that meant allowing them to make the occasional mistake.

If Josephine had led in that way, she would have supported her team, demonstrating her trust in them and their ability to support the business as she had. But, instead, Josephine struggled with trust.

For a leader, trust involves a difficult balance. Too little leads to micromanaging, which can inhibit growth, bring about self-doubt, or leave members of the team feeling frustrated or held back. Too much trust, as happens when a leader steps too far back, providing little oversight or involvement, can lead to poor decision-making, failure to meet objectives, and even power struggles among the team. Too much trust can also give way to rogue, de facto leadership. Josephine's issues were of too little trust. But both problems can largely be managed through proper mentoring.

Build Trust and Competency Through Mentoring

There are two types of decisions:
good decisions and lessons learned.

—Simon Sinek

Mentoring is a process that guides learning; it allows problems to become teachable moments. Rather than emphasizing an issue, you focus on the learning opportunity. Mentoring allows your team to gain knowledge and begin reaching their own conclusions. Unlike training, with mentoring, you are not telling; you are asking. You are empowering your team to think things through. Through mentoring, you build their capacity to make good decisions independent of your oversight.

Understandably, this has its challenges. While mistakes must be allowed, you may be hard-pressed to allow time to be wasted or errors to occur. There will be times when you can't help but intervene, ostensibly to guide your mentee or prevent costly blunders. But doing so interferes with the learning process and inhibits their growth. The more you intervene, the more likely your team will fall victim to the perils of micromanagement.

Rather than step in or dictate a process that has worked for you, honor your next-level leaders with the freedom to identify the right path. Start the process early on—before a costly mistake has occurred and your trust has waned. If you have a concern, ask questions. Help your mentee recognize the potential issue, then encourage them to revise their plan, taking that issue into consideration.

Allowing your team to identify the right strategy (even when you highlight the barriers or roadblocks you perceive) puts them in an active position. This inspires effort, fosters growth, and improves the likelihood that the learning will stick. Conversely, solving the problem for your team or imposing a solution will limit your team's learning and inhibit their ability to apply themselves and feel responsible for the outcomes they achieve.

Mentoring Improves Accountability and Trust

When there are weaknesses on your team, mentoring helps illuminate those gaps. Areas of weakness left unaddressed result in poor accountability, claims of incompetence, or both. These, in turn, beget conflict and tension among the team. Rather than struggle with these destructive elements, use mentoring to detect a lack of competency or commitment early on. The process of mentoring provides a healthy challenge to those on your team. It asks them to think things through and identify next steps. It, therefore, allows you to more easily determine if a member of your team is capable of learning and if they are the right fit for their role.

Think of mentoring as akin to teaching your son or daughter to drive a car. You know they need to learn lest you be left chauffering them for years to come. But you can't just give them a set of instructions and hand over the keys.

You begin with a discussion on the fundamentals of driving. You probably cover "what if" scenarios, explain the dangers and challenges of driving, and implore them with the overarching responsibility of being behind the wheel of a car. You might extend the conversation to cover automobile maintenance and the nuances of road conditions. But that is not nearly enough. Those initial discussions may occur before you even enter the vehicle.

So, you take your son or daughter on the road but maintain your role as the driver. You talk them through your choices on that excursion, pointing out things you'd discussed and those you'd neglected to mention.

Next, you become the passenger. Starting on a quiet and easy road, you watch your son or daughter's driving. You give pointers and advice. Gradually, you build them up to drive on more significant roads and highways. Your step-by-step process ensures they learn all they need and are ready to assume their new responsibility before being permitted (by you or the DMV) to drive a car independently. The process further allows you to develop trust in their ability, just as it permits them to establish trust in themselves. It enables you to discern when the essential skills have been acquired and gives you comfort that your child is ready to enjoy this new responsibility, free from your direct oversight.

The result of teaching your son or daughter to drive so they may enjoy more freedom and take on more responsibility is the product of mentoring.

Mentoring a member of your team to take on a new role or responsibility requires essentially the same dedication. You must talk it through, explaining your decisions and thinking. You must have them observe and ask questions. You must build them up gradually to take on more challenging terrain. You must trust them, and you must help them to trust themselves. There is no shortcut to good mentoring, just as there is no shortcut to teaching someone how to safely drive a car.

Mentoring sets you and your team up for success. It allows you to organically gain confidence in your team members' capacity to do the work. Reciprocally, your team members will be able to demonstrate their growing competency to you. As each member feels assured that you see their competency and value, they will increase their confidence, sense of security, and commitment to do the work. Everyone wins.

POINTS TO REMEMBER

Being a leader does not come with a promise of being trusted, nor does it come with a road map for developing trust in others.

This chapter provided you with food for thought and new strategies to FIX the trust issues impacting your leadership, allowing you to build a more trusting work environment.

Key Points

- The fundamental importance of consistency and predictability for building trust
- The transactional nature of trust and its correlation to maintaining a bank account
- That your team must believe in your competency and positive intentions as well as your care and concern for their growth and success
- The essence of mentoring and how it allows trust and accountability to flourish

This chapter also provided cautionary tales to illustrate the harm caused by some leadership tactics, explaining why to

- Avoid using the expression "Trust me."
- Reconsider the decision to praise publicly and criticize privately.

Trust is essential to the success of both the leader and their team. Yet, it does not stand alone. Trust and role clarity routinely overlap and become interrelated. Therefore, while trust is more foundational, it is essential that you understand how a leader's role clarity, or a lack thereof, can evolve into issues of trust.

CHAPTER SEVEN

ROLE CLARITY

A leader without a title is better than
a title without the ability to lead.

—Simon Sinek

Role Clarity is one of the most common aspects of the abyss or feedback gap.

Leaders nearly always believe they know their role and are clear about their responsibilities. Looking inward, do you feel confident of your ability to perform? Clear in your intentions? Consider how you relate to your team. Are you positive in your regard for others? Are you fulfilling your responsibilities to the best of your ability?

If I were to ask you those questions, I imagine you would have answered: Usually, yes, yes, and yes.

And yet, if you are like every other leader on the planet (you are), you miss things. You erroneously place blame on others. You neglect to see the steps you have taken that led to the problems at hand. You don't recognize which issues stem from you. Any concern you might have regarding your responsibility is quickly brushed aside as a product of your self-confidence and positive intentions.

The abyss, as such, is real. But it's not the fault of any one person. As a leader, you operate in your role with limited feedback and guidance. To fill any gap you perceive in your skills, you read books, join mentoring groups, enlist the support of a coach, or strive to follow in the footsteps of leaders you admire. But those efforts and outside influences are ill-equipped to pinpoint your gaps. They are unable to provide you with adequate guidance. Often, you are left unaware, and therefore you continue to make the same choices and mistakes. In some circumstances, a coach or outside influencer makes things worse.

> We were very happy that our leader had taken on a mentor, but it created a wedge because he would connect with his outside mentor for company decision making. He wouldn't rely on his executive team. We all wondered, "What are we here for?" And it was very confusing.
>
> I think that's where it took on both a trust issue and the role clarity issue because we really couldn't figure out what was happening.
>
> [Because the advice came from outside our team] we didn't have clear expectations from our leader. Ultimately, that resulted in the total lack of leadership. We were just floundering. No one was taking the lead.
>
> **H. Eisner**, Chief Operating Officer
> Company name withheld

Consider your internal team. As they are directly impacted, they may know there is a problem but may not recognize where the problem stems from. Should they have that degree of clarity (regardless of whether they are right or wrong), how likely do you think they will be to alert you to it? Unless your direct report is masochistic, a high risk-taker, or ready to leave their job, we can be sure that they would be reluctant to bring that information directly to you.

Can you rely on your HR team or peer group? Sadly, no. Similar issues exist with each. Should they be aware of the problem, your HR team will recognize that presenting you with such information poses a threat to their job security much as it would for your direct reports. Your peers, in turn, have little to gain and much to lose by pointing it out to you (and that presumes you have peers within the company *and* that your peers can accurately identify the issue). As a result, the information you need remains in the abyss.

Finally, your effort to develop in your role as a leader is limited because there exist only vague descriptors for what your role entails. The job description, should you have one, no doubt centers around reaching goals, leading meetings, acting as a liaison to the board, or being involved in an array of committees. But does your job description offer clarity or information about leading and managing others? Does it describe when or under what circumstances you need to get involved? Does it provide guidance on what to do in those situations? Does it set parameters around your leadership activities? I'm sure it offers no such detail or information.

Leaders, we know, are rarely given direct guidance on *how to lead*. Instead, an assumption is made that a leader understands and knows how to function in their new role. That means a tremendous part of a leader's role clarity is left open to interpretation. It needs to change.

Renowned leadership consultant and author Jack Zenger wrote a much-cited article, "We Wait Too Long to Train Our Leaders," published in *Harvard Business Review*. In it, Zenger reveals that in his research of some 17,000 leaders worldwide and across nearly every sector, that on average leaders receive their first leadership training at the age of forty-two. More concerning, Zenger notes, in those same firms the average age of supervisors was thirty-three and, in fact, the typical individual in these companies became a supervisor around age thirty. It follows then, says Zenger, that if they're not entering leadership training programs until they're forty-two, they are getting no leadership training at all as supervisors. And they're operating within the company untrained, on average, for over a decade. (Zenger, 2012)

Leaders simply don't get the support they require when they begin to manage and lead others.

To FIX many of the issues that stem from a lack of role clarity, let's revisit our leaders, Stuart, Gary, and Josephine, and identify how their issues with role clarity undermined trust and impacted success.

STUART – AUTONOMY IS NOT THE ANSWER

Stuart's notions about his role came largely from his concept of leadership, his observations of others, and the thin details he was given about what his role would entail. His job description identified who would report to him and provided him with information about his role as a liaison to the board of directors and his responsibility for connecting with organizational affiliates and other stakeholders.

What his job description didn't tell him was how to lead.

Stuart, new to leading a director-level team, based his leadership style on what he would want if he were in the shoes of his team: autonomy. Determined not to interfere, Stuart gave space to let the team do their jobs and trusted them. Having considered only the constructive aspects of autonomy, however, Stuart's judgment was clouded. When problems arose, he expected the team to handle those too. When a person infringed upon another's work or failed to be accountable to the others, Stuart didn't step in. In short, Stuart didn't recognize that his role as the leader would involve *actively* supporting his team. Not through telling them how to do their work, but by ensuring the team could work fluidly with one another.

The abyss Stuart faced stemmed from a lack of recognition that his role, on a somewhat granular level, would include removing hurdles, addressing conflict, and setting boundaries—that he would be directly involved in supporting the directors' work by eradicating the barriers impacting productivity or budgets. Stuart trusted his talented team to simply come together naturally and work out any emerging issues among themselves.

Establishing the Basics

Role clarity involves both the "what" and the "how" of a person's work. For Stuart and his team, the "what" of the organizational objectives was clear and agreed upon. All the directors knew *what* they were trying to accomplish and were genuinely committed to the goal. But *how* these objectives would be accomplished was not.

Each director on Stuart's team relied on their understanding of how best to achieve their interdependent goals. There was no unifying plan, no one person establishing how goals were to be accomplished. Stuart's team was like an all-star rowing team trying to compete in a race while their coxswain, essential for guiding synchronous movement and focus, remained absentmindedly on shore. An awakened leader understands that a profound part of their role involves creating a shared and agreed upon "how."

Setting Expectations
(to Guide Collaborative Action)

As the executive director, Stuart needed to initiate his relationship with the team and solidify his role as a leader by setting clear expectations for the group. These would have included clarifying individual and collective responsibilities, explaining how he wanted things handled, what information should be brought to his attention, etc. Stuart then needed to confirm that all members followed these established guidelines. Finally, Stuart needed to support the team in fulfilling the expectations he set. That would necessitate his checking in, getting feedback, refining expectations, and ensuring the team reached a point of fluidity in their work.

Had Stuart set those expectations, he would have recognized that collaborative efforts were being undermined by a single member of the team. He would have been aware of the need to engage directly with Oliver over the importance of communicating openly, attending meetings regularly, and running ideas and initiatives by the internal team before bringing them to outside stakeholders.

Affirming Your Authority (Stay Involved)

As a part of demonstrating his authority, Stuart would have been well served by attending all staff meetings, particularly in the beginning. The early formation of standards marks a pivotal point for any team. It is where essential structures and tone for the team are established. By being present, Stuart could have guided that process while providing initial clarity about roles, responsibilities, and boundaries. His continued engagement would have allowed him to identify the hurdles his team faced and remove the obstacles impacting their success.

JOSEPHINE – STEPPING UP AND LETTING GO

Josephine's issues with role clarity were nearly the opposite of Stuart's. Unlike Stuart, Josephine regularly engaged with her direct reports. She provided structure and guidance, attended team meetings, and supported a level of team interaction that ensured the fluidity of the work. Josephine's struggle with role clarity came instead from her deep roots in having developed the business. Her challenges with role clarity, familiar among legacy leaders, were fundamentally linked to her issues with trust. Could the company—and the team—survive without her direct oversight? Through her fears, Josephine remained not only invested but involved.

Josephine's staff members were aware of her long-term role and unquestionable knowledge at the company. They wanted to earn her trust and prove that they, too, could help the business thrive. That was evident when Jim, who had assumed Josephine's prior role once she became VP of Operations, would ask for her support and involvement rather than make the judgment call himself on a sticky issue. True to her nature, Josephine would provide guidance. When it seemed appropriate, she would also grant Jim permission to break with protocol. As a legacy leader, Josephine had the authority to do that. She'd helped establish those rules and therefore understood their purpose and where exceptions would be appropriate. But she was myopic in her support, forgetting that the rest of the team would be impacted.

Over time, the exceptions became routine, and protocol became meaningless. The lines between what is and is not allowed became blurred. It resulted in a domino effect. Jim became dependent on Josephine for managing the challenging situations. Her permitting the breaking of protocol, even as it compromised the work of others, led the team to believe Jim was favored.

Because she was an approachable leader, team members came to Josephine to voice their concerns. But Josephine's focus remained skewed toward the clients and keeping them happy. Her mindset was still linked to her prior role. With limited time and growing impatience, Josephine would dismiss her staff's concerns rather than bring resolution. Josephine's struggles with role clarity left her feeling overwhelmed with responsibility while leaving her team feeling unsupported and adrift.

Josephine's challenges are common among legacy leaders. While Josephine's intent may have been to support the team, she took away their ability to learn. As a result, they didn't become independent thinkers or accountable performers. Her involvement undermined the healthy collaboration she wanted to instill in the team.

Further, the shifting of protocol and resulting inconsistencies caused the team to lean on her more, not less, absorbing increasing amounts of her time and energy. If Josephine's directors had the skills or the potential, they were not developing them. While the company was doing well and growing, it was unclear if the current team would be capable of moving forward with it. Why? Because Josephine was too involved. She was holding all the strings, bolstering the work through her guidance. She was obscuring anyone's ability to see if these director-level staff were capable in their roles and preventing those staff from digging in and learning how to be successful. Due to her deep involvement, everyone was being held back.

Your Changing Role

Advancing as a leader is challenging, especially as you begin to establish yourself in that role. Your prior success most likely required a level of activity and performance measured differently from your current position. Your role may have shifted from client-centered to focusing on the internal team or external partnerships. As your responsibility has grown and changed, defining success has become murky. Your goals are now broad and require a team (or several teams) to deliver results. The heftier goals you shoulder require you to pivot in your role and shift your expectations onto others.

As the goals and responsibilities of your role increase, it does not equate to increasing the amount of work you do. You will not prove your worth as a leader by showing you can outperform your direct reports. Instead, you must leverage what you've learned and then help your next-level team develop those competencies.

Imagine you are the coach of a world-class athletic team. Since I know you are the best of the best, in this analogy, you're Phil Jackson. You've played ball. You've won championships. But now, instead of playing, you're coaching (leading) a team. Your job is no longer to get in position or have the team pass you the ball as the clock is ticking down. It isn't to fixate on what the fans, critics, or broadcasters are saying. It isn't to look important or be a showman. Your job is to lead your team to excellence by helping them perform at their best and to work *collaboratively*. Your role as coach and mentor is to create a dynamic where, as a team, they capitalize on their strengths, shore up their weaknesses, and in the end, everyone benefits. Your role as a business leader is no different.

When you are a leader over any team, whether newly hired or promoted from within, your first course of business must be to clarify your role related to those on your team. The team will also need that clarity to feel supported and engaged with their own responsibilities and to understand the distinctions of each person's role.

Developing Your Team

Assign tasks, and people will work for you. Assign responsibility, and people will work for themselves.

—Simon Sinek

The single most important thing you can do as an advancing leader is to prepare the team you lead to excel without your direct involvement. Beyond training, mentor them so that they become capable of performing the work and secure in their ability to do so. We've covered mentoring in our chapter on trust, but to recap, mentoring builds competency. Rather than stepping in to solve a problem, as the mentor, you guide learning and treat problems as teachable moments. You ensure your team gains sufficient knowledge enabling them to draw their own conclusions. Your purpose is to prepare and empower your team to make good decisions without your involvement.

Holding Them Accountable

Accountability, while deeply valued, is also profoundly misunderstood. We tie accountability to role and task assignment. The person appointed a task is responsible for the outcome and for achieving the desired result. That misses a key point: accountability requires control.

We saw this in our story about Josephine. Through her habit of micromanaging, she created a domino effect, compromising her team's ability to be accountable. It began with Josephine's support of Jim. Her willingness to step in and make decisions (including shifting of protocols) diminished Jim's sense of responsibility and limited his awareness over the outcome of those actions. Sheltered from any thought of the repercussions, Jim paid little thought to the impact his work would have on others. He offered no accountability to the other teams, instead behaving as if he was a cog in a wheel with no sense of control or direction.

But the shifting of protocol, even though authorized by Josephine, created unexpected demands on the teams downstream from his decision-making. It impacted their time and undermined their planning. Those groups had little control but tremendous responsibility for keeping the work moving and on schedule. The situation felt punitive and unreasonable. It built resentment, caused conflict, and resulted in the affected team members refusing to support the work. Josephine, angered by the resistance, became even more directive of those teams, lending the situation to even greater discontent. She didn't recognize that her actions were the foundation of the problem. She expected accountability, but she withheld control.

To offer a more simplistic illustration, consider your local weather forecaster. To predict the weather, ostensibly the core responsibility of their profession, your local forecaster incorporates satellite data, Doppler radar, ground information, and climate supercomputers. But should it rain on the day you've planned your outdoor wedding or event, you certainly couldn't hold them accountable. They simply have no control over the weather.

Building Accountability

Once you have developed and prepared your team, step back. Inform them of their responsibilities and grant them control. Permit them to find their skill level and identify where more learning is needed. Give them access to information and influence over the work.

Will they make mistakes? Of course. When they do, allow them to resolve it. Keep the responsibility with them. Have your team walk through their thinking, process what went wrong, and identify what needs to change. Should their actions impact other team members, much as was true of Jim's group, allow the team to discuss it among themselves. Encourage them to find a better process or the proper flow.

When your team is failing to demonstrate accountability, it is the result of limited control or a lack of responsibility for the outcome. Guide them toward getting each back on track, providing support where needed.

A capable team, free to perform their work without direct oversight or involvement, is the goal. Holding the team accountable, however, presumes that they want the responsibility and the control—that you've hired well and done the work of building up their capacity to become accountable. Building accountability is the responsibility of the leader, not the employee. It is so core to a leader's success that I've devoted Chapter 12 to that purpose.

GARY — KNOW YOUR LIMITS

When Gary began his role as dean of studies in a large department of a university, he had over 100 faculty and their support staff and administrators reporting to him. He was wise to create structure and boundaries so that he could manage and support his team. Yet, Gary's concept of the leader's role was far from perfect. The boundaries he created were flawed and inappropriate. Gary didn't understand the limits of his role.

Gary created a chain of command but didn't honor it. Instead, he usurped the authority of his direct reports, meeting privately with members of their teams. Those "open-door" meetings were shrouded in secrecy. Gary's intention of protecting his direct reports by making plans and changes without garnering their input or involvement had the opposite effect. He left his direct reports vulnerable, shouldering the responsibility and the blame for changes they did not make. Gary's actions created a growing and vicious cycle of confusion and gossip. He did so while believing his actions were quelling the drama. Gary was deeply in the abyss when it came to role clarity.

Gary's concept of his role stood in stark contrast to healthy leadership. Kind-hearted and magnanimous, Gary encouraged others to come to him with their issues and concerns. He wanted to connect with them and to support their needs. Gary failed to recognize, however, that his effort to be helpful and engaged was usurping the authority of his division leaders. He didn't consider that he needed to be inclusive in his decision-making nor that bringing forth change without consulting those directly involved would be problematic. Gary's desire was for connection with the faculty. What it led to was confusion, commotion, and chaos.

Chain of Command

Had Gary respected his chain of command, much of the conflict could have been avoided. Had he engaged with his division heads, Berniece and Andrew, before making changes, he would have understood the challenges and problems those changes would beget. He would have been informed about the value and purpose of the committee appointments he was influencing. He would have known why certain faculty members might rightfully retain their office spaces, even if it was incongruent with his plan. In short, Gary would have benefited from Andrew and Berniece's historical knowledge of the people and their personalities. With the support of his team, Gary would have learned how seemingly altruistic requests were being made out of self-interest. And he would have had the benefit of their insight for recognizing that his surface-level solutions were destined to produce deep-seated problems.

Beyond avoiding much of the chaos and discontent caused by his actions, Gary would have found that by empowering his division heads to contribute to the conversation or lead in this decision-making, he would strengthen his role *and* theirs. Had he retained the chain of command as his division heads wanted, the issues which grew and plagued the entire department would have been easily contained.

Establishing Roles

Role clarity involves both how you establish and how you maintain the chain of command. While the expression "chain of command" can seem prickly as it suggests a domineering or authoritarian leader, the concept is both important and necessary, even in today's more flattened organizational structures. Each team member needs to know where they fit and where they do not. Without a clear chain of command, many employees could feel lost.

As a leader, others report to you. Typically, it is to get your input or approval on activities relevant to their role. Occasionally, it may be to get your help or support in overcoming a hurdle or resolving an issue. A chain of command ensures that your team members know who to talk to when they need support or are ready to move forward on a collaborative project. It creates a clear path for keeping a team on track and productive. Regardless of what you call it or how you feel about it, a chain of command provides a clear path for support while also preventing anarchy within the company.

As a leader, you may communicate with the whole company or large segments of the staff. However, certain aspects of communication are reserved for your immediate direct reports. This is *your* team. Their work directly supports your role. In turn, you must support them in *their* role, which means establishing and securing their role and authority, allowing them to appropriately lead their teams.

Surviving a Disruption to the Hierarchy

Part of managing the chain of command includes managing your interactions with those who do not report to you. Yes, employees who don't report to you will occasionally seek your guidance. It may be that you are more approachable, their leader is unavailable, or they simply do not like the answer their leader has given them. Sometimes, it may be appropriate to engage with those members of your organization, but there are parameters. Your willingness to engage must still prevent the situation from undermining the established hierarchy and creating disruption.

Before you engage in problem-solving or further discussion with a staff member leaping up the chain of command, have that person divulge why they are coming to you. It may be possible to redirect them to a more appropriate source. If that is not the case, and they have a discernible reason for bringing an issue to you, inform the person seeking your counsel that the information, and any decision you make, will be discussed with their supervisor.

The exception to this, of course, would be if the complaint or reason they are seeking your counsel is due to concerns about that supervisor or how that supervisor might treat the issue being presented. In such cases, partial or complete confidentiality *is appropriate* for protecting the employee voicing the complaint. I'll cover this further in Chapter 11 on Managing Conflict.

After speaking with the staff member seeking your counsel, do as you said. Follow through and communicate the conversation with their supervisor or leader. That supports the organizational hierarchy, the supervisor, and the individual employee. You support the employee's effort to bring resolution or closure, and you do so without undermining or blindsiding their leader. You are closing the loop by keeping the parties aware and involved.

Unfortunately, I've seen leaders of remarkable competency disregard these basic guidelines. Some do so out of expediency, others out of a shared disrespect for the leader who is being usurped, and some leaders are genuinely unaware, as was the case with Gary. Regardless of the reason, the behavior can be read as unprofessional to inappropriate. Further, it sets a dangerous precedent that invites continued disruption to the chain of command.

PROVIDING TRANSPARENCY

Gary kept everything close to his vest when it came to making decisions. Perhaps he did not believe the division heads or faculty would respect his authority should he allow them access to his decision-making. Regardless, Gary's efforts to protect the faculty led him to provide confidentiality where it didn't belong. Even though he saw his role as protecting members of the team who voiced concern, in effect, his efforts put the entire team in jeopardy. His lack of transparency led the team down a path of confusion and frustration and precipitated the gossip, rumors, and claims of favoritism that followed.

While, as a leader, you are free to make decisions, you must also consider the impact your actions have on others. Sharing the reasons behind your decisions serves several critical purposes.

First, it allows your team to identify problems or concerns they see, including something you may have overlooked or not fully considered. Ironically, this is the reason some leaders avoid sharing. They don't want naysayers. They view sharing information as a threat to their leadership, interfering with their ability to be trusted to make good decisions. But the opposite is true. Sharing demonstrates your leadership. You aren't asking permission; you are rounding out your idea, identifying gaps.

Second, keeping group members informed creates collaboration and support of ideas. They can ask questions, learn what's expected, understand why something is necessary. That, in turn, promotes buy-in, teamwork, and productivity. You are increasing the team's knowledge and readiness for the change.

Third, when you are transparent and openly share information, you develop trust. You allow your team to see behind the curtain and know what is happening and why. Conversely, holding on tightly to all information, innocuous or not, breeds concern.

Finally, engaging your team in determining the best solutions builds support of your ideas and demonstrates inclusion. That, in turn, builds meaning to the team's work, enhances collaboration, and models appropriate skills in both communication and leadership—behaviors that are important throughout the chain of command.

Like accountability, transparency reflects trust, role clarity, and conflict management.

POINTS TO REMEMBER

Most leaders engage in one or more behaviors that interfere with role clarity. Some, as the leaders in our stories, have a gap in their awareness that leads them to engage in their problem behavior habitually. Others may have some awareness yet still engage in the actions occasionally or under certain circumstances.

You may look at your leadership role and recognize only a glimmer of this. You may dismiss the importance of examining your role clarity in that you rarely compete with your team, make decisions without keeping everyone informed, or usurp the authority of another member of your organization. Do not dismiss the importance of these lessons, even if your slip-ups are rare. Any infraction, however minor, creates a deep and lasting impression. It colors your image as an authority, indicates a diminished level of maturity, and, most concerning of all, undermines your team's ability to trust you.

How you embody your role demonstrates your trustworthiness to your team. The level at which you perform, therefore, requires consistency and unwavering responsibility. Without it, you undermine trust and damage your relationship with your team.

KEY POINTS

As a leader, you are not only responsible for managing the roles of others; you must also manage your role.

- Others cannot, or will not, alert you to gaps in your role clarity.

- Your role establishes and maintains the collaborative action of your team.

- Developing your team to perform without direct oversight allows them to become accountable.

- Honor the chain of command; it is an essential part of supporting the roles of others.

- Be transparent in your decision-making, particularly in offering the "why" behind your actions.

Mastering your role as a leader allows you to develop and deepen the trust of your team and improve productivity and growth for your company. When you possess good role clarity and demonstrate confidence in each team member, they can control their role, and accountability is the result. Strengths within your team quickly become apparent, and weaknesses can be addressed. You can focus on the larger picture of the business.

While trust and role clarity are critical elements of healthy leadership, they are not enough. Unexpected issues will still erupt. Frustrations and tension will percolate within even the most cohesive of groups. Supporting your team through such challenges is also part of your role. How you handle those disruptions will further establish, or erode, the trust they have in you. Therefore, the final key component of healthy leadership is managing conflict.

CHAPTER EIGHT

CONFLICT MANAGEMENT

Every conflict we face in life is rich with
positive and negative potential.
It can be a source of inspiration, enlightenment,
learning, transformation, and growth—or rage,
fear, shame, entrapment, and resistance.
The choice is not up to our opponents,
but to us and our willingness
to face and work through them.

—Kenneth Cloke

Most leaders' efforts in conflict management begin only after conflict has erupted, although tensions had been simmering long before.

When conflict erupts, efforts to identify and resolve the conflict focus on those believed to be causing the tension or making the complaints. It seems logical. They are the obvious choice; they are involved in the conflict. But this is a mistake. Most often, the issues underlying the conflict are not their fault. Those involved are experiencing tension or acting out their frustrations, but the causative factors, and therefore the changes that are needed, almost always reside elsewhere. Most often, they live at the leadership level.

E. is not a confrontational person. He was just never going to put himself in a position of having a difficult conversation if it could be avoided. His method of resolution was to continue to step further away from the group and focus more on his corporate responsibilities. For somebody who had been a significant presence in the office for twenty-some-odd years, it looked like he simply was withdrawing. It created some concerns about his role. About whom and what to trust.

M. Sullivan, Managing Principal
Company Name Withheld

To better understand how conflict evolves and manifests itself, we'll look at how this happened with Stuart, Gary, and Josephine and the changes they, or you, need to change to fix the dynamic.

STUART — HEALTHY BOUNDARIES REMOVE BARRIERS

Having selected and hired his team of directors, Stuart found it easy to trust in them. He knew each could be exceptional in their role. He firmly believed that with passionate, talented, and capable employees, building a healthy foundation was all he would need to do for the team to succeed. Bring in the best and then get out of their way.

Leading a team is somewhat like conducting an orchestra. Each member is necessarily focused on their role—their part. But the leader, like a conductor, must create the symphonic result. Just as a conductor must determine when each player comes in, how loud and how long they play, and how they exit, a leader determines the collaborative activity of the team.

Stuart did not act as a conductor. His core value of autonomy was fundamentally linked to his challenges in managing conflict on his team. He didn't account for the fact that people can never be perfectly aligned— that we are all given to making choices others wouldn't make and that we must therefore learn to navigate alongside one another. Stuart didn't recognize that trust alone would not eliminate tension.

When a member of Stuart's team crossed boundaries, stepped onto others' turf, and didn't accept the boundaries set by his peers, the heightened tension needed resolution. It required the support of the leader. But Stuart was ill-prepared to handle it. While Stuart said he would attend to their concerns, the team witnessed no noticeable change. Considering the circumstances and the limited information from Stuart, the team didn't believe he was supporting them. The problems they were experiencing due to their colleague were not getting resolved.

Stuart wasn't providing adequate support, yet he asked his team to trust him and have faith that it would get better. When things didn't improve, and the team took matters into their own hands, they found themselves being chastised by Stuart. The team's irritation and growing anger quickly transitioned. The conflict was no longer static or fixated on Oliver. The team was focused on Stuart.

Supporting the Team

Stuart's mistake was that his vision of autonomy extended into his response to conflict. But, by not stepping in, supporting, or protecting his team, he left them feeling exposed or isolated. Some became detached from the bigger picture and less committed to the work. Frustrated team members were also given to becoming myopic, focusing more on the issue or problem person than organizational needs.

The challenge of conflict is that even those outside the core issues are impacted. Beyond the noticeable disruption, they will sense the tension or find the resulting behaviors create a distraction or otherwise obstruct their work. The situation soon becomes uncomfortable for everyone, unbearable for some. As a result, those impacted will inevitably seek to create change. Stuart's team did that when they took matters into their own hands.

As a leader, you need to be both willing and able to address tension and conflict occurring on your team. For example, Stuart could have demonstrated a willingness by being available to his team, inviting them to share their concerns, listening for signs of discontent or friction, and asking questions (even generally) about how he could support his team. Stuart would then have needed to take action to demonstrate his ability to address the conflict. We'll get more into managing conflict later in this chapter. The problem is that Stuart and many leaders like him are either unwilling or unable to address the tension and conflict on their team. When that happens, it will inevitably grow, eventually destabilizing everything—the group, the leader (you), and the organization.

Removing the Barriers to Success

Stuart was correct in many ways. A leader doesn't need to structure or micromanage his team. Trust and autonomy are appropriate and expected. But a leader does need to remove the barriers to success.

Barriers to success include interference from outside parties, limitations due to a lack of information, or a shortage of necessary supplies. It can be created by internal members of the team (as was the case with Oliver in Stuart's situation), leaders of other teams, or a board of directors. Barriers can also be caused by customers, vendors, other external stakeholders, legislative or political issues, and even sweeping concerns like the weather or a pandemic. While a leader can't control all barriers to success, he must at least acknowledge them and their impact on the team. More importantly, when an issue is within a leaders' purview, such as those brought about by internal influencers and organizational events, a leader is expected to address it. The leader's role is to remove the barriers to success. Failing in this capacity erodes trust. A leader's ability to manage conflict directly impacts their role and reputation.

GARY – SHARING KNOWLEDGE PREVENTS ASSUMPTIONS

In restructuring his department, Gary's efforts in conflict management were geared toward containment. In stark contrast to Stuart, Gary invited those frustrated or concerned to come directly to him. He assured them that he would listen and, where possible, fix things. Well-meaning and good-natured, Gary believed that by engaging and understanding his team's needs, he could provide whatever support they needed. He presumed that the issues would be simple and the solutions straightforward. Given his authority and good intentions, Gary believed he could resolve team concerns without much ado.

Gary had begun his tenure as dean by making substantial changes to the large university department where he served. He instituted an open-door policy as an outlet for any discontent those changes brought about. To appease the safety concerns of those coming to Gary to broach an issue, he provided confidentiality. However, Gary's seemingly innocuous and kind efforts led to confusion, chaos, and increasing complaints. They disrupted boundaries and gave way to escalating conflict.

Transparency Minimizes Conflict

Like many leaders with a possessive approach to information, Gary unwittingly created conflict among those confiding in and reporting to him. Such leaders believe they are protecting their team, prefer to keep things on a need-to-know basis, or don't consider what information might be essential to share. Regardless, their reluctance to be inclusive leads to tension and conflict. Uninformed employees are left to draw their own conclusions about the purpose or rationale behind a change, decision, or edict that comes down the chain of command. They are likely to engage in back-channel communication, snooping, and other endeavors to fill the vacuum of information.

All that inevitably leads to assumptions and causes false information to be circulated. Gossip and rumors are quick to follow, and conflicts will inevitably escalate. We saw that clearly within Gary's department, where secrecy led to rumor and fear settled in. The relationships among the faculty quickly unwound as self-protective side-taking and silos took over. Employees and the company alike incur the damage caused by withholding information.

Providing information and being transparent with your reasons, rationale, or purpose behind decisions allows employees to clarify the bigger picture and their role in it. It opens communication and creates an easy opportunity for your people to put their concerns or issues on the table for discussion. It also gives them access to your motives, which could otherwise be misconstrued.

Stuart and Gary, as well as their respective teams, suffered due to a lack of transparency. Both leaders were given to saying, "Trust me." Each failed to recognize the dynamic they were creating, particularly when their efforts did not address the issues they purported to have resolved. Stuart's team continued to be impacted by Oliver. Gary's team routinely saw changes that (for them) lacked reason. Had either been open and forthcoming with their efforts and intentions, their respective teams would have known what was being done, why it was being done, and where to bring concerns.

Be Inclusive with Those Impacted

While providing transparency is the goal, you may wonder, how far does that reach? Surely, everyone does not need to know everything. The rule of thumb is this. Keep those affected by your actions involved. Yes, there will be differences in the extent of your transparency. Even a company-wide initiative may involve varying degrees of disclosure depending on the role of any particular team. The level of disclosure should be closely tied to the level of impact on that team. Similarly, a person's level of seniority can dictate a different level of access to information.

Nevertheless, including those affected is essential for mitigating and preventing conflict. By sharing information and broaching a discussion, you allow individuals to be informed, feel included, and, if needed, to voice concern. Rather than have their worries expressed behind the scenes where the flames of concern can be easily fanned and spread, you can tackle emerging issues head-on.

I've noticed that one prevalent gap among leaders is that they lack awareness about the significance of sharing information. You can find it in all three of our stories. Each one offers a glimpse into the pattern where a lack of disclosure leads to problems. Nearly every client I have encountered has grappled with issues resulting from this lack of inclusion.

While a leader must be free to make some decisions without collaborative input, it is nevertheless essential to communicate about the reasons behind those decisions, allowing those impacted an opportunity to engage. The more significant the impact on any individual, the more they need to be included in the process.

Consider Gary. He made changes to committee appointments, office locations, and reporting structure. He offered clarity about the reasons for the reporting structure and how he divided the faculty. While many were frustrated or displeased, and some complained, it did not lead to conflict. The reasons were clear, and they were shared.

However, Gary did not engage with those impacted by his other decisions, such as shifting committee appointments. Therefore, the affected parties were left to speculate not only about why the change was warranted (sometimes it was obvious) but who had requested it. It was easy to form conclusions based on who benefited, but those assumptions were often incorrect. Gary's need-to-know basis was wholly inaccurate. Those who needed information were prevented from receiving it. The ensuing frustration and anger quickly gave way to finger-pointing, tension, and conflict.

Stuart's lack of transparency and inclusion was evident in his concealing details about his effort to address the team's concerns over Oliver. Stuart had elected to manage the issue privately out of respect for Oliver. While this was appropriate as an initial approach, once it became clear that change was lagging, Stuart needed to protect the sanctity of his team by disclosing information about the efforts being made. Stuart, however, believed he could take the heat. He said, "Trust me," expecting that would be sufficient. He didn't want to be the leader who threw a member of his team under the bus.

There is a more measured response than what Stuart considered—one that protects all participants. But it requires identifying when and why to hold your corrective conversation in public versus in private.

Public or Private Discourse?

When a team member is creating disruption, it necessitates your attention. It is your responsibility to manage and defuse the friction or conflict being created.

Stuart was correct in beginning this effort privately, but he made the mistake of keeping it there. The two main parameters indicating that it is appropriate to keep a corrective conversation private are 1) it is the first time you are discussing it with the team member, or 2) the issue is only affecting that team member, and no one within the organization has expressed concern. The latter would include a performance concern or a situation where a client or vendor has voiced a complaint. At that point, your role is to make your team member aware of the problem. Your perspective here should be to vindicate not villainize; to believe that your team member is not willfully creating conflict or problems and that they are not fully aware of their impact.

When you share this information privately, you allow your team member to retain their dignity. By holding the perspective to vindicate not villainize, you provide them with the benefit of the doubt. That allows them to bring change without further embarrassment. This effort builds trust and can resolve the conflict without further ado. It bears noting that there are also times when it is legally required that you engage in the conversation privately, such as for issues related to health or other personal information as protected by HIPAA.

But there are times when the conversation must leave the private realm. For example, you've addressed the issue privately, but no change has been observed, and the team continues to be impacted by the behavior (and is therefore awaiting change). At this point, it's time to adjust your strategy. Your effort to expand the conversation and include the team is not to embarrass or punish the person at the core of the problem. Instead, your purpose is to open a dialogue to bring about necessary change. The "side" you are taking is cohesion. Your goal is to get your team functioning fluidly. In Chapter Thirteen on Critical Conversations, I list ten reasons for managing an issue or conflict in a team format. I've also provided a robust description of how to introduce and conduct that team meeting. For now, just recognize the importance of these corrective conversations on managing conflict and the impact they have in affecting trust among your team members.

Managing Exceptions When Transparency is Limited

It's important to share information with the team, particularly when the data has a bearing on them. However, there are times when you may need to filter what you share. That is the case when divulging too much information has the potential, or likelihood, of causing a profound financial or legal impact. When such issues are at hand, you play a vital role in addressing the lack of transparency and managing the expectations of your team.

Below we'll explore situations of this ilk that arise from company-wide issues, think of merger and acquisition activities or impending layoffs, as well as smaller intimate issues, where HIPPA might limit the sharing of information. I will provide you with guidance on how to filter the level of transparency without sacrificing trust with your team.

In a perfect world, you would openly share planning, discuss concerns, and explore possibilities in collaboration with your team. The honesty and transparency of that effort would cultivate a feeling of safety. Your team members would not need to guess at your (or the organization's) intentions, goals, or efforts, so gossip and rumors would be nonexistent. The information would be readily provided and confusion minimized. With this level of transparency, many elements that lead to conflict would be prevented.

Company-Wide Issues

Situations of great magnitude, such as a merger, an acquisition, or impending layoffs often signal a time of secrecy. Leaders have private meetings and make decisions directly affecting their workforce, often while never breathing a word. Employees, as a result, are caught off guard when the information is revealed. Some may feel betrayed. Others may have made financial commitments, such as buying a house or planning an expensive vacation, which they would not have made had they had access to the information. There may even be times you knew of their plans to make such commitments and yet said nothing.

While there is an unquestionable impact and cost to the employees in these cases, there also remain substantial reasons to keep the details private. Nevertheless, you have a responsibility to engage with your employees once the change has been revealed. Even if they are angry, the team deserves to receive full disclosure about the reasons surrounding the decision and the secrecy. Why was the change needed? What other options had been attempted or considered? What are the intended benefits of the change? Are more changes anticipated?

Change that impacts us, especially when it blindsides us, creates stress. By openly sharing information and offering background details, you will help bring understanding and closure. Your efforts will help assure your team that they are no longer in the dark and will further illuminate the reasons for any prior deception. Addressing your team's concerns, even if not explicitly, is essential for bringing them back into a place of trust.

Small or Intimate Issues

Sometimes situations are more intimate and require a degree of opacity, even though they are likely to have a direct impact on other members of your team. For example, consider the changes you would need to make to accommodate a health crisis or personal circumstance affecting a member of your team. You may need to adjust the work hours, expectations, and job responsibilities of the whole team to maintain productivity or manage customers. Here, you may be privy to the personal information of the employee who is unable to perform as expected, and their situation may directly impact your decision-making. Yet, you are unable to share your reasons for bringing about change. However, while specific details are privileged when an employee's health or personal status is involved, you can disclose the broader scope of the change and the reasons behind it.

For example, say you have an employee, Sarah, who has been put on medically restricted duties. While it is certainly within your purview to change the roles or expectations of your team without providing an explanation, it will likely come at a cost. For one, if your team is unaware of the reasons for the change, members will naturally draw their own conclusions. Shielding them from information gives way to gossip, which can easily lead to incorrect assumptions. They may get the idea that Sarah is favored or is about to be fired.

Therefore, sharing your rationale for the change is essential. You can say, "Sarah has informed the company of a personal situation that will interfere with her ability to work forty hours a week. We expect this to last about three months and anticipate Sarah will then be resuming her role in its full capacity. So, for the next three months, we will be making the following changes . . ." As the leader, you have given essential information to your team about the impact and expectations, yet you have not divulged any privileged information.

The more clarity and information you share, the greater your ability to achieve cooperation from the team, which, in turn, will instill the team's confidence and support.

While there are legitimate, even legally required, reasons for withholding information from a team, there is still a cost for that exclusion. Therefore, as an awakened leader, opt to disclose what you can, even if it's simply to explain your inability to share more. The key is to refocus the team on what matters most for *them*: the direct impact on their work, any expectations that have changed, and how the changes will be managed in the short and long term.

JOSEPHINE – A "TEAM VIEWPOINT" IMPROVES INDIVIDUAL ACCOUNTABILITY

Conflict on Josephine's team was a byproduct of her struggles with role clarity and her micromanaging of the group. She frequently ignored protocol, and her decision-making process was uneven. These actions blurred the lines of responsibility, undermined accountability, and created the appearance of favoritism among her team members. Josephine's effort to manage the conflicts that began to percolate only made things worse. Josephine didn't invest time in identifying the causative factors. Instead, she attended to it by giving her team directives.

While less dramatic than that with Stuart or Gary's teams, conflict on Josephine's team was still damaging. As frustrations expanded and were left unaddressed, Josephine's team (much like Stuart's) took issues into their own hands. Maya refused to accommodate the fluctuating timelines caused by Jim's team breaking from protocol. Her resistance created tension between her team and Jim's. This breakdown in the process culminated in a loss of talent, client dissatisfaction, and undermined the collaborative spirit Josephine saw as essential for organizational success.

Creating a "Team Viewpoint"

Members of your team must understand not only their specific role, goals, and objectives but also know how their role interrelates with that of all others on the team. Deliberately focusing on a team viewpoint will help set the team's guiding principles and define each member's expected and appropriate actions. Moreover, it is imperative that you, as the leader, adopt this viewpoint. When any member of your team is negatively affected by others, it creates an impact. The result is individual conflicts and team disruption. Your actions are what determine the team's recovery.

As you reflect on this point, consider how Jim's behavior impacted his team and the resulting fallout. When any member of your team is negatively affected by others, the behaviors and interactions of the entire team must be examined, discussed, and adjusted as necessary. If not, conflict will most certainly grow.

Support Role Responsibility

Having clarity on roles would have been instrumental in preventing conflict on Josephine's team. Imagine if Jim had adopted full responsibility for his position. The team members impacted by his circumventing protocol would have approached him directly to share their concerns.

Similarly, rather than looking to Josephine to grant him permission, Jim would recognize the need to engage with the broader team to discuss the situation at hand.

Communication among Josephine's team would be more robust with this balance of responsibility. The conversation among the group would allow Jim insight into the impact of his work on others.

Likewise, the team would understand any dilemmas Jim was facing. Together, they could discuss and debate the merits of a situational change in protocol, or the greater team could provide Jim with guidance on how to move forward if the change wasn't warranted. This inclusive decision-making process would have fostered cohesion and clarity as they managed the situation together.

The team's collective effort manages the conflict and reduces tensions by building team members' understanding of one another. It creates agreement while taking the onus of finding a solution off the leader. Same-level team members will gain clarity of the knowledge and capacity of their colleagues. As this happens, those they report to will be afforded the opportunity to recognize who among their team is reactive versus forward-thinking. For a leader, this process of managing conflict strengthens the team and provides clear evidence of who among the group could become the organization's future leaders.

This is such an important point that I want to repeat it. Managing conflict, by creating a team viewpoint and building role responsibility, strengthens your team and provides you with clear evidence of who among the team has the capacity to become future leaders of your organization.

Granting Authority Builds Responsibility

To see your team take on greater responsibility, you must be able to let go and grant your team the authority to find solutions. The change does not need to be abrupt. While removing yourself entirely might be the ultimate goal, there is an intermediate step. Take on the role of an observer. In this capacity, your role is to support respectful disagreement and sharing concerns while relinquishing control for making decisions.

Stepping back and acting as an observer provides you with a vantage point to see and hear your team's needs and concerns, while still conveying that they have the responsibility for making decisions. As an observer, you would be present to weigh in where needed while maintaining the distance to recognize who among your team possesses the knowledge, vision, and wisdom to work independently of your oversight. It allows you to assess their readiness for having autonomy.

This shift also prevents a significant amount of conflict. When all members of a group have an opportunity to share their concerns and speak of the harmful impact or positive results expected, it creates a more unified vision among them.

Your team will understand resistance when they recognize the impact it has on others. They will appreciate a team member's persistence when they are made aware of the benefits or limited alternatives for achieving the same outcome. By having a heightened awareness, your team can resolve their own conflicts and create their own solutions. They will be more willing and better prepared to provide help or support and to lessen the impact on those most affected.

That was the transformation Josephine and her team experienced. Coming together led them to a broader awareness of not only the client's wants but each other's concerns. The group began to work out solutions together, and conflicts quickly subsided. Through quiet observation, Josephine's role transitioned to bearing witness rather than acting as judge and jury. She was better able to trust her team and their ability to solve problems collectively. It freed her to focus on the more global aspects of her role.

Bringing Change without Causing Conflict

Josephine and Gary each had team members who approached them privately to request action or change. They both engaged with their team member and, based on those conversations, decided on the best course of action and instituted the changes they deemed necessary. Neither Josephine nor Gary included anyone else before making their decisions. And it led to conflict.

When your actions or decisions directly impact another person, it is imperative that you include that person in your decision-making process. It's a critical step in preventing conflict. Gary would have avoided most of the conflict that erupted within his department if, rather than promise confidentiality, he had expressed the need to discuss the issue with the other person or people involved. Josephine likewise would have prevented conflict among her team had she taken the time to engage with Maya and the other impacted directors before permitting Jim to break from protocol.

Whenever a member of your team raises a complaint, it is essential that you learn the perspective of those involved before drawing a conclusion or creating any change. Remember, vindicate; don't villainize. Whatever led to a complaint, you can be sure the person complaining has a valid reason for doing so or isn't aware of the circumstances surrounding the problem. Either way, engaging directly with the person at the heart of the complaint is the only way to determine the source of the problem or its solution. Only with this information can you bring about change without bringing about conflict.

Conflict management is inclusive and involves open communication. Open communication informs, adds clarity, and builds your team's awareness of each other's role and contributions. Similarly, you will become aware of the impact and needs from all sides. Being inclusive gives voice to the team for determining outcomes because it allows you to listen without an expectation of decision-making. While still involved, your role will be to pose thoughtful questions or guide learning. In this capacity, you have the added benefit of observing each person's ability to communicate effectively, process new information, and show growth and understanding. Altogether, this process puts power into the team while strengthening both team and leader.

POINTS TO REMEMBER

Your responsibility for managing conflict on your team is as important as building trust and as relevant as understanding your own role. Managing conflict is part of your role as a leader and cannot be passed off to your HR team or other conflict resolution professionals.

Your ability to manage conflict is reflected in how you step up, show up, and stand up for your team. The respect you receive from your team will be directly linked to how well you support them.

Conflict management begins well before a conflict erupts. Your ability to stay in front of it depends first on your role clarity—your awareness that managing flow and disruption on your team is a critical part of your role. And second, it depends on your ability to gain the team's trust such that they know they can rely on you for aid and support. Your ability to influence change when conflicts arise, fundamentally requires both.

KEY POINTS

- As a leader, you are responsible for establishing and maintaining boundaries and removing barriers to your team's success.
- Your role is to ensure your team can work effectively together.
- When there is change, be transparent and inclusive. Ensure that those impacted are aware and (whenever possible) involved.
- Create a "team viewpoint" to ensure others understand the interrelated elements of their role and the impact of their actions.
- Recognize that not all corrective conversations should be private. Sometimes, a corrective conversation must be held with the team.

A leader's skill in managing conflict has a direct impact on their reputation and an indirect but profound impact on their level of success.

CLOSING THOUGHTS ON FIX

In "FIX," we focused on the actions and decisions leaders erroneously make, which inevitably undermine their authority, derail their success, and harm the organization they serve.

By looking at the situations each of our leaders experienced, I exposed the missteps and mistakes each made with their respective teams and showed how those errors in judgment led to conflict, upheaval, loss of talent, and other concerns.

Though each story involves vastly different circumstances, all three illuminated the need for trust, role clarity, and conflict management. Those three pillars of successful leadership became the focus of FIX.

Starting with trust, I moved through each of the three pillars for success and identified the areas each leader needed to FIX and the specific changes the leader needed to make in order to keep that particular pillar strong.

In FIX, you had the opportunity to learn vicariously through those stories, identifying any necessary changes to your behavior and learning what it takes to successfully lead and support your team—what it takes to become a self-aware and successful leader.

In our chapter on trust, I explained what builds and what destroys trust in a team. I also covered why using the expression "Trust me" is a fatal mistake. While discussing the pillar of trust, you learned about creating a "trust account," the importance of transparency, and why mentoring builds accountability.

Moving into role clarity, I covered the importance of embracing the changes to your role as you progress up the chain of command, and I described the primary functions of a leader. You learned about the delicate balance of your authority and about the damage caused by granting too much or too little autonomy. Role clarity focused on a leader's role in building a collaborative team.

Finally, in our pillar on conflict management, I explained the value of being approachable to discuss issues of conflict and disruption on your team and why you might choose to address an issue privately or publicly. In our chapter on conflict management, you learned why change requires transparency and inclusivity, and how to manage expectations when that is not possible.

The FIX segment was critical to your learning the steps you need to *stop* taking, and what to do instead. Simply avoiding pitfalls, however, is not nearly enough. In the next section, FILL, we will shift our focus to the proactive efforts you can begin to make to build trust, enhance role clarity, and properly manage conflict.

The section about FILL will serve to fill your strategy bucket with new ideas and information. Let's get started!

PART FOUR

FILL

INTRODUCTION TO FILL

Welcome to FILL! I hope that you've arrived at this section of the book having already learned to FIND the issues impacting your leadership based on the behaviors you are seeing within your team. And that you have discovered steps to FIX the problematic behaviors you have been engaging in, thereby solidifying your leadership. As you have found and fixed those gaps in your leadership, it is appropriate to begin learning new behaviors that can FILL your remaining leadership gaps.

A word of caution if you are starting your read here. Suppose you begin implementing the strategies I share in FILL without first understanding which current actions you need to stop engaging in (through FIND and FIX). In that case, you are likely to demonstrate inconsistencies that create added stress and confusion for your team. In essence, you would be attempting to build a new structure on a damaged foundation. It will undermine your efforts and potentially create damage to your team.

In FILL, we build on what you've learned so far. It will provide you with insight and teach you new strategies and behaviors to build trust, establish role clarity, and appropriately manage conflict on your team.

Unlike the other sections of this book, FILL begins with role clarity. As you understand the role you are meant to play for your team and how to lead them, the concepts of trust and conflict management flow more naturally.

In FILL, you will learn how to establish your role as the leader and ways to support each team member in their role. You will learn how to develop and maintain trust, even when trust has been damaged or is at an all-time low. Finally, you will learn how to manage and prevent conflict among your team members.

CHAPTER NINE

ROLE CLARITY

We can't be good at everything.
If we were, there would be no need for teams.

—Simon Sinek

I've found conversations surrounding role clarity to be the prickliest when working with leaders. I have yet to meet a leader who doesn't push back at the notion that they aren't doing exactly the right things or making the best choices and decisions in a particular situation. Indeed, each leader thinks they are. You do too. I have no doubt that you have tried to do all the right things—that you care about your team and want to support their success. As you consider the gaps in your current leadership, remember my mantra: vindicate; don't villainize. Be kind to yourself.

But stick with me; there are parts of your role that you are probably not fulfilling. Do you have staff reluctant to voice their concerns or share their misgivings about a project? Are there complaints, issues of gossip, or rumors? Have you seen problems go unaddressed or conflict build? Then you have seen the result of leadership foibles. My focus isn't about shame; it's about change.

Role clarity is thoroughly intertwined with both trust and conflict management. Trust issues underlie silence, the failure to voice concern, and possibly the reason for citing a complaint. How conflict is (or is not) managed underlies your team's relationship with one another, the boundaries they hold, their ability, and their willingness to work with one another. The way you manage your role has a tremendous impact. It dictates the trust you obtain and the conflicts your team can overcome.

Consider this: do you accept responsibility and adjust your role when matters of trust or conflict arise? As issues surface, do you act or do you push back, directing the problems elsewhere? Are there times you ignore those troubles altogether, preferring to focus on the work instead?

I've seen leaders take each stance. I believe they move in those directions for two reasons. They either lack the requisite skill for managing conflict or lack awareness of their principal role as a leader: to support their team's success.

Having clarity about what your role as a leader requires is essential. Unfortunately, as we've already discussed, most companies offer a stunning lack of support in preparing their supervisors, managers, and leaders to form the skills and awareness they need.

This chapter serves to correct that belief by illuminating the foundational concepts of leadership and filling that gap.

This is the role of a leader, in its simplest form :

- Identify goals.
- Set the direction of the team.
- Remove obstacles to success.

Most leaders excel at the first part, at identifying goals. You are most likely in your role because of your vision and ability to delegate. You know what you want your team to achieve, and you have a vision of what lies ahead. Setting the direction for your team is usually straightforward. You share the goals, tell the team your expectations, and await their success.

The problem is that your role as a leader goes beyond identifying goals and setting the team's direction. It extends beyond growing the business or expanding the team. Your role is essentially to create a platform of success for others.

As you climb in your career, you must release aspects of each prior role. At one point, you went from worker to manager. While still performing some of the work you once did, your time was divided. Part of it became overseeing the work of others, ensuring their performance is strong and that they can be successful. Each step up the chain of command draws you further on this path of ensuring the success of *others*. Many leaders struggle along this path when they lose sight of *their* role in the organization's success—their role in supporting the success of others.

A Change of Perspective

The traditional organizational chart is partly to blame for the challenges of leadership. It places the lower levels of the team at the bottom, supporting the higher tiers. Visually this makes the most sense. There are fewer at the top. Top suggests best. But this creates an unrealistic viewpoint.

If you flip the visual and consider the chart inversely, you find that each manager, director, or leader, supports those directly above them. You see your role as ensuring that your team can fulfill their roles. This visual identifies the heavy responsibility of those in management and leadership. It provides the rationale for the increased compensation. As you consider that along with the responsibilities you shoulder, it probably resonates with you. It also serves as a reminder of the importance of ensuring your team can do their part. Things they overlook or ignore will no doubt fall on you.

Your Role in Removing Obstacles

Your role as a leader is to support your team:

- Eliminate hurdles.
- Create healthy boundaries.
- Appropriately manage stress points or conflicts.

If you fail to take responsibility for any of these, it will impact the team and compromise the work they perform.

Hurdles and barriers arise when your team lacks clarity about the expected results, has received inadequate preparedness (training or mentoring), insufficient time, materials, information, or even connections. Hurdles take shape when someone or something is interfering with progress and success.

Your role in eliminating hurdles begins before any task is assigned and before any project is underway. It requires preparing your team for success.

Ensure you provide them with adequate materials, time, information, and connections to others involved. Provide each member with clear details about your expectations. Finally, stand ready to prevent or resolve any interferences that may arise.

I've found that leaders who do not support their team in this way are prone to describing the issues that later arise as being related to accountability.

Accountability, however, requires both control and responsibility. While individual members of your staff may be responsible for an outcome, these circumstances arise because they have limited control. Your role is to step in and provide information, support boundaries, and remove obstacles. If you do not, and issues like these are not addressed, they inevitably morph into workplace tensions and conflict.

Initial problems arise when a leader is not supporting boundaries or removing hurdles yet keeps expectations high. The heightened stress and aggravation among the team invariably leads to finger-pointing and blame, which are second-level problems. When leaders fall short of managing first-level problems, the team stagnates. When they dismiss second-level problems or inadequately resolve them while still holding the same expectations, they set their team up for failure.

While you may not see your role as connected with these entanglements, it is. Your role as a leader, and your opportunities for success, are indelibly tied to this principal role of supporting your team by addressing their obstacles. Acknowledging the problems and addressing things early on is key to prevention. Chapter Eleven, Conflict Management, will cover this in detail, teaching you specific strategies to help you manage conflict when first-level circumstances have escalated to second-level problems.

Preparing the Team for Success

A broad part of your role as the leader is to create a space of fluidity for the work, to remove hurdles and make success possible for everyone on the team.

Therefore, your role is upheld when you have prepared your team for their responsibilities and provided them with adequate control so that they can perform at their best.

Ensuring that each team member can be responsible requires adequate training and mentoring. Training provides the "how" of the work, including nuances of the task and essential things to be aware of. Mentoring provides a deeper understanding of the "why" behind the work.

Mentoring is the longer-term part of the growth arc. Mentoring allows the trained employee to develop into a capable and knowledgeable member of the team—one who can process information deeply, predict outcomes, and course-correct without further guidance. As we discussed in Chapter Six, unlike training, mentoring conversations are guided by questions rather than answers. They may include the following: What might happen if you . . .? What have you learned from . . .? What needs to change? Mentoring is an ongoing process. It builds your team's capacity to think ahead, prepare for what's next, and (one day) lead. The better you train your team, the more you can trust they can do the work. The better you mentor them, the more you can rely on the results.

Recognize Where you Have Control

Leaders often resist giving their team complete control or authority over their work. Considering the organizational chart formed with an inverted triangle, the reasons seem obvious. Leaders will avoid giving full control if they believe the problems will fall on them.

The challenge for most leaders is that they exert control in the wrong places. They exert control over deliverables and outcomes but not over obstacles. They want to prevent problems and fallout but focus on the efforts or productivity rather than the issues interfering with the team's success.

Remember our story of Stuart? His team struggled and the organization suffered due to the rogue behavior of one member. Stuart's team attempted to bring change on their own, but they were unsuccessful. Without authority, they lacked the power to alter their circumstances. They were expected to take full responsibility for the problems while they held no control over what or who was causing them.

As a leader, supporting your team includes taking charge of the problems that impact them. You have the authority and the control to discipline or terminate a member of the team. For that reason, evaluate each problem, complaint, and concern through the lens of accountability. Consider whether the person who is struggling is failing to take responsibility or is simply lacking in control.

New Beginnings

Creating a new beginning on your team starts with communication and transparency. As you have considered your role and identified things you will be changing, plan to alert your team to those changes. The same holds true if you are a new leader over an existing unit.

Tell your team about the changes they can expect to see. Redefining roles, including your own, is not something that should be done silently or discretely. Bring your interest in creating change to your direct reports before taking any steps in the change process.

Any change you intend to make—be it your strategy for managing conflict, building trust, or modifying your role—should be done openly and transparently. That builds trust. Saying what you are going to do before you do it demonstrates sincerity and follow-through. Your team becomes engaged when you forewarn and prepare them. They feel valued and included in the journey that lies ahead.

If you think you can make a change so seamless that others won't notice, I offer this note of caution. When something changes, even slightly, others will notice, even if they cannot pinpoint what or why. Withholding information prickles with secrecy builds suspicion and damages trust. Don't do it.

Instead, share your concerns about maintaining the status quo. If you have made mistakes, own them. If it was a prior leader you have taken over for, remember to vindicate not villainize that leader. These efforts are purposeful. When you own your mistakes, you model honesty, ownership, and responsibility for bringing about change. But if you blame others or focus on the negative, you alert your team that you are likely to adopt that tone or behavior with them or their work. In so doing, you only encourage them to hide mistakes and problems.

Adam Grant, best-selling author of *Think Again, The Power of Knowing What You Don't Know* tweeted about this: Saying, "I was wrong" isn't an admission of incompetence. It's a sign that you have the humility to recognize your mistakes and the integrity to learn from them. The faster you acknowledge when you're wrong, the faster you can move toward being right. (Twitter, March 3, 2021)

Focus on learning rather than failure. Demonstrate the type of leader you will be. Help your team feel safe approaching you with a mistake by seeing your focus on learning and looking forward.

In her best-selling book, *Dare to Lead*, Brené Brown talks about the transformation this effort had on her own team.

"At first people were hesitant to believe that we were serious about the no shaming or blaming. But over time, they started to speak up in meetings. Whether it was asking the question without knowing the answer, or sharing the outcomes from an initiative that had underdelivered. Formerly talked about as failures, now reframed as learnings.

"Once we removed the fear of failure and the fear of being judged, we started to outlearn, and outperform our best competitors." (Brown 2018)

As you work to establish a new platform of trust, include your team in the process. Outline your ideas for change, then engage your team by inviting them to further those ideas through a brainstorming process. Redefining your role in this manner enhances the strategies for building trust. By demonstrating inclusion, you create buy-in and build collaboration, both of which are necessary to support your effort to restructure the roles and responsibilities of the team.

Getting Comfortable with Change

Being a leader means being comfortable with change. Making a shift in your role begins with determining what you will relinquish or take on and how that transition will occur. Questions to consider include these: What knowledge must be transferred? How long will the training and mentoring last? What introductions and connections need to be fostered? And what will your role look like afterward?

That final question—identifying what happens next—is often the doozy. Leaders often deeply enjoy elements of the work that no longer fall within their purview. Giving up that responsibility may seem unpleasant or even unthinkable. I've heard leaders explain their reluctance with statements like: *The client needs me; I've always been their connection. I understand their problem (or needs) best. This is a high-profile client; I should handle it.* While each statement may be true, and the client may indeed want you, that doesn't make it the right thing to do.

Once you've been elevated to a role that no longer explicitly includes a day-to-day level of client service, taking on clients as special cases sends a damaging message to your team and the client. The group notices you are openly competing with them. Your involvement suggests you make an unflattering comparison of their work to yours. Further, by maintaining day-to-day client engagement, you are less available to maintain your role of creating a platform of success for your team.

You are less able to support your team by eliminating hurdles, creating healthy boundaries, and appropriately managing stress points or conflicts impacting the team's work. *These* are your roles as a leader. Your decision to continue working with a client is also a disservice to the client as they are left to believe that you alone are capable of supporting them. Moreover, given that your actual role holds many other responsibilities, the client is likely to experience your lack of availability and conflicting priorities.

Finally, the company's growth and success would be undermined by this behavior. By taking on the work, you are passing on opportunities to mentor your team and abandoning your role as a leader. You are not building the business or determining the plan and path for the future when you hold tight to your prior role. Yes, it may feel right at the moment. But staying accountable for a role that is no longer yours is holding you, the client, your team, and the company back.

When you embrace your role as a leader, you will find new responsibilities fill your time. Instead of the intricate aspects of client work, you will discover opportunities, attend to longer-term efforts, and influence the sway of the business. Those are your roles as a visionary. Your next role is more grounded and is what we've spent the majority of this chapter discussing. It is the role of supporting your team, being available to them when they encounter a hurdle, either inside or outside of the group, and supporting healthy change so you can all succeed.

To FILL your gaps as a leader, you must first acknowledge that the gaps exist, and second recognize that they are essential to fill.

This chapter on role clarity does not chastise you for what you don't know but acknowledges what you have not been taught and what no one is telling you.

KEY POINTS

- Having clarity on your role is essential, as it defines how and why you build trust and manage conflicts among your team.

- As a leader, you must let go of old responsibilities and relinquish duties that should instead be the responsibility of your direct reports.

- Supporting the people reporting to you is essential for ensuring individual and collective success.

- Supporting your team means eliminating hurdles, creating and supporting healthy boundaries, and appropriately managing any stress points or conflicts impacting their work. With this support, your team can deliver on the expected outcome.

One way to better understand your role as a leader is to invert the traditional organizational chart. A leader's role is to support the work of others.

CHAPTER TEN

TRUST

A team is not a group of people who work together. A team is a group of people who trust each other.

—Simon Sinek

They See Who You Are

Trust involves authenticity. Others notice when you walk your talk and how you show up in a situation. It takes many interactions because trust develops as others see how you act and learn how you respond to different circumstances. Trust develops when there is predictability.

As a leader, your team has undoubtedly formed an impression of who you are. They know if you are conflict avoidant or heavy-handed, helpful, or disengaged. They know if you praise their efforts or shame their mistakes. They have observed you countless times and have heard stories about you from others. Their memory and read on things may be different than your own. Nevertheless, it determines their predictions and their expectations of you. It determines their trust in you.

Who you are is a byproduct of how you behave and treat others, what you decide, and what you value. It's both what you share of yourself and what others notice about you. Altogether, these inform your team on a visceral level of how trustworthy you are. Your success as a leader hinges on your team seeing you as trustworthy.

Building Trust

David DeSteno, a professor of psychology at Northeastern University and the author of *The Truth About Trust,* points out that one of the most effective trust-building strategies is to create a personal connection. Yet he reflects, "As a person's power increases, their perceived trustworthiness goes down." DeSteno recommends counteracting this view by getting to know the people on your team, openly accepting responsibility for mistakes, and being consistent. He emphasizes that to build trust; people need to know that they are dealing with the true you. (O'Hara, 2014).

How can you develop trust with your team? While there is no formula or magic bullet, I have identified four essential factors in building trust. Conversely, where there is an absence of any of these factors, trust is hindered.

There are four tenets of trust:

TRANSPARENCY

HONESTY

OPENNESS

RESPECT

The acronym here is THOR. As you may know, Thor was a Norse God of thunder, weather, and crops who had a mighty hammer that he used to create storms. But Thor was also known for providing strength and protection. Think of these four qualities— Transparency, Honesty, Openness, and Respect—as having the power of Thor. In their absence, they create storms, and with their presence, they demonstrate strength and provide protection.

TRANSPARENCY – Transparency is, at its core, the fearless sharing of information. It relates to trust as it is about being forthcoming with knowledge, reasons, and information. It requires vulnerability as it demonstrates the importance of taking responsibility and acknowledging missteps. An honest and transparent discussion will shed light on deeper thoughts or information. It helps your team be prepared for what may come and learn from things that don't go as planned. Transparency helps your whole team make better, more informed decisions.

Most leaders offer varying degrees of transparency. For example, you may admit you've made a mistake but not disclose the details. Or say, "We're pivoting and shifting gears," but not explain why. These are surface-level efforts at transparency and do not build trust. They leave your team with unanswered questions. When you are genuinely transparent, there isn't much need to ask questions as information is shared and available for discussion. True transparency means you share more than what may be required, not less. Your team feels secure in asking a question should one come to mind and confident that you will provide an answer. They trust you want them to be fully informed and aware and that you will respond to them openly.

Transparency is, at its core, the fearless sharing of information. Transparency, as a tenet of trust, is broad and thorough. When you are transparent, you allow others to know what you are doing and why you are doing it. You invite them to share your perspective and build their understanding of you and your decisions. Transparency provides your team with an opportunity to question or challenge, just as it provides you an opportunity to respond to your team's concerns and deepen their knowledge.

Transparency develops trust and breeds reciprocity. As you trust your team, they will trust you. As you openly share information, so will they.

HONESTY – Transparency and honesty are deeply intertwined. Where transparency will be seen through your open sharing of information, honesty is identified by taking responsibility for your actions.

Your honesty is demonstrated by admitting mistakes, sharing doubts, and being self-reflective. In conjunction with transparency, it offers revelations and acknowledgments, taking ownership when it's hard and crediting others when they succeed. Honesty, as such, requires vulnerability. As others experience your vulnerability, they notice you trust them. Your willingness to trust builds feelings of reciprocity, informing your team that they too can be honest and vulnerable. *They* can trust *you*.

When you value honesty, your leadership is demonstrated not through perfection or bravado but through taking responsibility and providing learning. To borrow my favorite lyric from the Jason Mraz song, "I'm Yours," we all *win some or learn some*.* Mistakes are key to success. They build our ability to grow and learn. Your leadership shines through your ability to recover from mistakes, take different actions, and bring better results.

---

*Excerpt from 'I'm Yours' by Jason Mraz, 2008 used with permission

Conversely, by denying or concealing a mistake or placing blame elsewhere, you limit the learning not only for yourself but for your team as well. Further, if your team is aware of your deflection or cover-up, you damage your reputation with them. You undermine their trust in you. Whether or not others find out, denying or concealing a mistake places your team in jeopardy of being held responsible or making other unnecessary mistakes. Your lack of honesty undermines them.

Fear of vulnerability leads to secrecy and the covering up of a mistake. It not only inhibits learning but models this behavior to the team. Hide mistakes, never show weakness. These are the qualities that will bring everyone down. We know these stories. They carry names like Enron, Wells Fargo, and Lehman Brothers. They led to the banking collapse of 2008 and the Sarbanes-Oxley Act in 2002. (In case you're interested in reading more about these, links are provided at the end of the book in our references section).

Vulnerability is not weakness. Author and researcher Brené Brown speaks and writes extensively on the topic. She defines it in her book *Dare to Lead*, "Vulnerability is not winning or losing. It's having the courage to show up when you can't control the outcome" (Brown 2018). Vulnerability is both honest and brave. It allows you to expose a problem and explore alternatives. It's inclusive by its disclosure. While your honesty may be identified by your vulnerability, your leadership is defined by your ability to address the problems that have been revealed, rise above them, and continue to move forward with vision and direction.

In a blog post based on her book, *Radical Candor: Be a Kick-Ass Boss Without Losing Your Humanity*, author Kim Scott emphasizes the value of building a culture of self-criticism on your team. She tells leaders to lead by example by admitting mistakes and crediting others in front of their team. She recommends leaders take it a step further, explaining why they made such an admission. And she recommends leaders encourage their teams to similarly take ownership for a mistake.

Scott shares a simple technique she calls "Whoops-a-Daisy" to encourage ownership and diminish the embarrassment of admitting a mistake. Scott bought a stuffed daisy and put it in front of herself at each all-hands meeting. She then asked people to nominate themselves for a "Whoops."

In exchange for confessing to some mistake, they would be granted instant forgiveness. This shifted the culture and helped prevent others from making the same mistake.

Honesty is a tenet that the leader must uphold for it to be assumed by the team. As you show up with your team in an honest and forthcoming manner, you are modeling the behavior for them. Your actions and attitude guide theirs. If you want your team to be responsible, accountable, and own their mistakes, be a role model who builds trust through honesty.

Internationally recognized author, poet, and social media sensation Beau Taplin famously wrote about *Lies & Silence*. "Lies and silences carry their own kinds of truth. You can learn a great deal about a person's character and motives through what they choose to withhold from you."

OPENNESS – Openness serves to round out the tenets of honesty and transparency. As the counterpoint of transparency, which involves a commitment to *offer* information and answer questions, being open connects with *receiving* information from others. By being open, you encourage others to share and, more importantly, show your willingness to hear divergent ideas and opinions. When you display this quality, you grant others a degree of comfort and safety in asking questions or challenging a decision. You provide them with an opportunity to share their perspective, ideas, and information.

Being open encourages collaboration. Your team learns that it is safe to share ideas and perspectives. That offering feedback or critique can be done respectfully. When a leader is transparent, honest, and open, it creates psychological safety—safety to take risks, express ideas, or share opinions without fear of repercussions. As we discussed in Chapter Six, with psychological safety, those on your team feel more confident admitting a mistake, asking a question, or offering an idea. When you model and inspire openness, you create a team with high psychological safety and foster an environment where everyone learns together.

With psychological safety, employees feel safer pushing themselves and risks seem smaller because the team trusts that others have their back. Being open means decisions are collaborative, and everyone learns together. When you engage in and support this ideal, your actions demonstrate to the team that each is valued and that their contributions are recognized.

RESPECT – While I'm bringing it up last, respect is the foundation upon which healthy relationships are built. Your team notices how you treat others. It goes beyond being kind or using an appropriate tone of voice. Respect is deeply connected with the other tenets of trust—the consistency with which you are open, honest, and transparent. These, in combination, have a far more significant impact on the level of respect felt by your team.

Your team will feel respected when you acknowledge and praise good work and strong efforts—when you listen to them and look them in the eye—when you respect their concerns and respond to their needs. They will feel respect when you ensure that they are treated fairly by you and others. They will feel respected when you correct them without criticism and when you support them without micromanaging their work. They will feel respected when you are honest about their strengths and shortcomings and are willing to tell them the truth to help them be better. These are the result of transparency, honesty, and openness.

Respect creates the environment for trust to grow and flourish.

Putting the Tenets Together

When people on your team feel respected, they are willing to show up. When they believe you are being honest, they are going to listen. When you are transparent, they will look deeper. And when you are open, they will tell you what they think.

When you and your team have trust, you will excel farther than ever before. It is only with trust that you can truly have each other's back. Trust occurs when you know one another's weaknesses, and rather than exploit them, you support them where they need it most.

With all four of the tenets of trust (transparency, honesty, openness, and respect), your team will be solid and collaborative. They will support you and each other. They will be accountable and prepared.

Let's put this concept into action. Say you have an idea or a plan taking shape, so you pull your team together. To be thorough, you provide your team with a broad perspective, essential information, and possibly some nonessential details. After sharing your thoughts with the team, you ask for their input.

Far from feeling unnerved by your having engaged them, your team rejoices in the opportunity to contribute. Familiar with the collaborative role they play, your team asks questions, pokes holes in your ideas or solutions, and furthers your thoughts around the subject. Their engagement works to support you, just as yours served to include them. Your team has helped vet the now-well-rounded idea. Before committing to a specific action or decision, you achieve greater clarity and garner team support.

Without this level of interaction and inclusion, you're likely to find your team holds back and makes no more than a tenuous effort to point out a flaw, offer an idea, or help find a solution. By having trust and using THOR to engage your team as active participants in determining the right plan and solution, your team is ready for what's next. Their buy-in is full.

Rules and Limitations on Personal Disclosures

While building trust relies upon being open, honest, and transparent, there are limitations on where these are appropriate. For that reason, it is important to discuss the concept of personal disclosures more fully, especially as they relate to trust-building.

I've worked with a handful of leaders who want to demonstrate honesty and build a relationship with their team but who do so by divulging random aspects of their personal lives or simply oversharing. These do not lead to their desired result. On the contrary, at best, their behavior seems unprofessional. At worst, it comes across as anything from strange to insincere to grossly inappropriate.

There are also leaders I've met who occupy the other end of the spectrum. These leaders don't believe in mixing the personal with the professional and resist sharing anything about themselves, preferring to minimize social interactions with their staff. Neither of these actions is healthy nor will they develop trust with your team. One lacks boundaries, while the other withholds too much.

I recommend the following rule of thumb. To develop trust among those you work with, share information that has relevance to the work (THOR), is common knowledge or basic information about you (for example, that you are married, have children, or drive a BMW), and share personal information that has a life-altering component.

Why those things? The first two are straightforward. As I described while covering the tenets of trust, THOR is the professional and work-related sharing that develops trust. Enough said. When you are forthcoming with basic personal information, you show that you are human and create a sense of commonality to those who have similar lives. The final circumstance where I recommend sharing, where the information is life-altering, is essential because any impact on you may bring reverberations to the workplace.

Consider, for example, that your child is sick or your infirmed parent is coming to live with you. You may be out of the office and unavailable. This has relevance in the workplace, and the team should know essential information around it. They should know what's happening, why, and what to expect.

On the other hand, perhaps you are getting married, having a baby, or something else of life-altering impact is happening in your world. These are important to share, even if you can argue that they will not impact the workplace. They are essential to disclose because of their great significance *to you*. Your reluctance to share this positive information will come across as untrusting or unfriendly when it comes to light (and it always does). Holding back is likely to create a hurdle that impacts your relationships and people's willingness to work with you.

Certainly, there are exceptions to the rule. While life-impacting situations have the likelihood of creating an impact in the workplace, no, you are not required to share. But, when there is an impact on others, sharing some basics allows others to move forward. They know what to expect about your ability to work, anticipated return if you are away, etc.

Building trust in the workplace does not mean personal disclosures. Beyond the situations I've just illustrated, honesty at work is *not* related to your personal life. It is related to THOR As such, any personal disclosures should be limited to that realm.

Creating A Fresh Start

As you become a more awakened leader, you may recognize the need for transforming your relationship with your team or within your organization. You now know trust is not where it needs to be. You want to hit the Reset button. You may be wondering, *Is it possible to start over and rebuild?* The short answer is, yes, it is possible. Better still, the process doesn't need to be daunting. The *method* in which you reset trust simultaneously initiates the process of transforming trust as it currently exists.

Your first step is to identify what you, as the leader, need to change. Do you need to be more open? Honest? Transparent? What aspects of your leadership style need to change? Getting clear about your responsibility is an essential first step. Creating clarity around this is vital as your efforts to rebuild trust will include sharing these revelations with your team.

Second, open up communication with your team about your intended change. Speak of your desire to build trust with them. Acknowledge your past shortcomings in being THOR Be specific of your missteps, but do not elaborate with examples.*

Share with them your reasons for wanting to make a change and speak of the efforts you will be taking. That begins to demonstrate that you are worthy of their trust. By openly sharing this intention, you are demonstrating your effort and commitment to being more honest and transparent in real time. That will begin to ignite your team's belief that your desire for change is legitimate.

In some situations, especially those where trust has been badly damaged, or there is a lot of water under the bridge, you will need to be more specific. You need to own the mistake(s) you have made.

For example, consider our story about Gary. If Gary were interested in transforming the level of trust on his team, he would need to specifically address his error in making departmental decisions without garnering others' input and usurping his established chain of command. Gary would not need to address any individual circumstance but rather the global issue.

Perhaps you inherited a group or team that was already untrusting. Either you were brought in from the outside, or you were promoted to replace a leader who has left. You may want a fresh start, but the team does not reset its trust in leadership just because there is a new person in the chair. Their negative experiences are not forgotten, and they do not evaporate.

Your actions to bring about change will need to be similarly engaging as if you had damaged the trust yourself. Just as the leader who is remaining

---

* By remaining general, each person can accept the information with his/her own example in mind. The distinction of what will be different determined by their own experiences.

with his team, you will need to begin by acknowledging that the team has suffered and is not ready to trust. Let them know that you want to work with them to create a positive change, get their buy-in, and start where they are. Identify, with their help, what went wrong in the past. Then build on that knowledge, sharing your plan to do things differently. Speak of and demonstrate the differences in your leadership. These initial steps are essential, enabling the team to consider that your desire and ability to create change are legitimate.

Regardless of the cause and whether it predates your leadership or not, when trust is damaged, repairs are needed. No one can instill confidence or build a relationship over a chasm of distrust. That means not only acknowledging the current status—including, as appropriate, your own responsibility for creating it—but also explaining what led up to it. As you share that information, you exhibit transparency and provide your team with another glimpse of your sincerity. Perhaps more to the point, this act is essential for creating a change in your team's ability to form trust.

For trust to occur, we need to reconcile it with the past. We need to understand it, learn from it, and make peace with it. Only then can we move beyond it.

Understanding the Fluidity of Trust

Trust is fluid and able to change. But one's ability to accept the change as real is based on their own past experiences. Trust evolves as a product of our experiences and is determined based on our expectations of the future.

I want to build on the concept of fluidity as it relates to trust, so I'll use an analogy of water. Like water, trust flows. Both carry a degree of predictability but will behave differently depending on the conditions. Both can just as easily support us as crush us.

Consider then that our trust in another person builds much like a layer of ice does over a body of water. The ice starts out thin, and if conditions are consistent, it builds. In the beginning, you know the ice is thin, so you avoid stepping on it. Soon it can support small things like a bird or a rock. But it can hold nothing substantial. It would be treacherous to step on that ice, and you would be foolish to trust in its ability to support you. Over time, the ice has built up. It is stronger and has been around longer. It may appear safe to tread upon. Perhaps at this point, someone you know has decided it looked safe enough to walk on and gave it a try. They stepped onto the ice, and they fell through.

Regardless of the impact that the experience has on them—perhaps the situation was relatively minor—it has colored *your* view of the safety of that ice. That is especially so if you had shared in their judgment and believed the ice was strong enough to support them. Your ability to trust that ice, and even your judgment of it, is irreparably altered. You won't choose to walk on that ice unless there is a powerful way of identifying when it is safe to do so. You need information. You need to know what led to the ice breaking and what made it dangerous so that you can make a safer choice. Trust is about learning what is and is not safe.

Applying this analogy of water to that of trust on your team alerts you to the necessity of explaining the thoughts or circumstances that underlay past decisions and actions. It signals why it is important and even essential that you specify how (and why) things will be different to the team. These steps are integral to the team's learning to place their trust in you. Short of that clarity, you are asking them to trust that the ice will support them even when they have no reason to believe that it will.

POINTS TO REMEMBER

Trust is built or destroyed by the small interaction, not the grand overture. It grows slowly and requires attention and maintenance. But given time, it gets stronger and can support you. It builds opportunities for greatness.

Building or FILLing a gap in trust is essential for creating a healthy and collaborative team. And it's up to the leader to develop it.

KEY POINTS

- THOR – Transparency, Honesty, Openness, and Respect are the four critical elements for building trust. While THOR involves reciprocity, it can only succeed when it starts with the leader.

- Trust can only be developed on a solid foundation. Problems, issues, and misdeeds of the past must be owned and resolved before trust has room to grow.

CHAPTER ELEVEN

CONFLICT MANAGEMENT

You have planned for your career, promotions, and retirement. You have prepared for company growth, created strategies, and formed alliances. You have built teams, developed strategic plans, and participated in mergers and acquisitions. But have you ever *planned* for conflict? Have you ever formed a structured plan for managing the unavoidable struggles that arise when people work together—for ensuring that destructive conflict is minimized and the flow of work unhampered? The best way to prevent conflict and mitigate the damage it may cause is the same as with any other anticipatable hurdle or problem: to have a plan and be prepared to deal with it.

Everyone, whether in a personal or work environment, experiences conflict. It's a normal, even healthy part of our human development as it helps us grow and evolve. We push each other, intentionally or not, because we have differing visions, ideals, preferences, and opinions. These differences can challenge our thinking and push us to work harder. But they can also cause stress, silos, and lead to breakdowns in collaboration and productivity.

Conflict will always fall into one of two categories: constructive (the building up of ourselves and others), or destructive (the taking down). In business, where we need to ensure that our teams work fluidly and collaboratively with one another, where the success and possibly the business's survival may rest on the health of the employee interactions, it becomes essential that we manage the conflict. How conflict is handled will largely determine the outcome, whether it is constructive or not.

Adam Grant offers a great description of the differences between constructive and destructive conflict in his book *Think Again*. In it, Grant differentiates task conflict from relationship conflict. Task conflict, he explains, occurs when a group of people disagrees over ideas or opinions. In that situation, it is easy for the group to remain united; to work together in resolving a problem. In contrast, relationship conflict occurs when disagreements focus on personal qualities or attributes; when a person is viewed as being responsible for the problem. While the latter type of conflict can tear teams apart, the former is an essential part of effective teams and partnerships; it builds trust and allows team effectiveness to grow.

While developing a plan for managing conflict may sound painful or unpleasant, it is not as hard as you think. The nuances of any individual conflict are not important. Rather, the structure and preparedness are what matter most. A thorough plan will include strategies for conflict prevention, management, and resolution.

The sections that follow will help you to create your successful plan. In the first section, I'll help you craft a strategy for preventing conflict. The core elements for conflict prevention will tap into the skills covered in previous chapters: trust (along with the related aspects of inclusion and transparency) and role clarity. In this section, I will touch upon them again to connect the concepts. Moving past prevention is a section that provides guidance for managing conflict as tensions begin to rise. In the final section of our conflict management planning, I share some of my top strategies for resolving conflict once the issues have escalated.

STRATEGIES FOR PREVENTING CONFLICT

Foster Trust throughout Your Team

When trust between you and your team is strong, you are well poised to prevent conflict among those on the team. Fostering trust *between* members of your team is even more valuable.

Trust among your team will become evident when your team is open to feedback, owns their mistakes, and listens to one another—when they share a common effort and support one another. You, as the leader, hold a defining role in determining the relationship of those on your team. It begins with you. By modeling trust, rewarding it, and fostering it, you help develop an interrelated trust among your team members.

As a leader, your behavior sets the standard. To prevent conflict, it is essential that you foster trust.

Show Your Care

Beyond any outward demonstrations of trust, your team will feel secure when they know you care about them, value their work and contribution, and sincerely want them to be successful. For these reasons, a trusting team will come to you with a problem. They trust you will guide and support them in getting the situation resolved. They have no fear that you will mock them, shame them, or brush them off. They engage with you to address the problem before it spins out of control or impacts the work. You can prevent conflict from erupting because you learn about it before things escalate.

Openly Commit to Being Helpful

To increase your odds of success, let everyone know of your desire to be supportive *before* a problem arises. Let your team know that their ability to work fluidly is important to you. Be sure they know that if there is an interruption they cannot resolve on their own, you want them to come to you.

I use the word *interruption* over *conflict* as we are talking about prevention. Your choice of words indicates to your team when you want them to reach out for assistance. Encouraging them to reach out when there is an *interruption* allows you to be privy to the issue early enough to prevent a conflict from developing.

Beyond your words, demonstrate your commitment through actions. Let your team know how their issues will be addressed, for example, will you have a team powwow to discuss it openly? And always follow through.

Model Inclusion and Transparency

Preventable conflict often occurs because of a lack of information. When you shield your employees or hold too tightly to information and control, you create an opportunity for back-channel communication. Your team, aware of missing details or information, will naturally seek to fill that void. Their effort to understand what is happening or why quickly leads to gossip and rumor. This all-too-common pattern will undermine the team's trust in you and create or magnify factions between groups.

The solution for preventing conflict that arises from these situations is straightforward: include your team in planning and decisions. Be forthcoming. Offer more information than your team might need, not less. Invite them to ask questions, voice concerns, and share alternate perspectives.

Your transparency builds trust and aids in your team's understanding and acceptance of things that are happening. Your actions also model the behavior for those on the team, teaching them to be inclusive and transparent with one another. Your efforts, copied and emulated by others, will help to mitigate and prevent conflict.

Ensure Clarity – Everyone Plays a Role

Role clarity identifies who does what on the team. It has a bearing on the flow of work, communication between group members, problem identification, accountability, and more. It is how your team works together.

Ensure each member of your team has complete clarity about their role. Guide them with information that reaches beyond tasks and deliverables; discuss how their role intersects with the rest of the team. Among the most preventable conflicts arise when team members inappropriately rely on others, fail to be accountable to one another, or don't recognize the need to engage and collaborate with others. These issues evolve out of a lack of role clarity.

Set and Uphold Boundaries

Your role necessarily includes creating a pathway to success for your team. Pay attention to how team members work together. Take an active part in assuring your team's success. Prevent conflict by setting, monitoring, and upholding boundaries.

When there are barriers, even those not occurring internally, knock them down in support of your team. Your role in preventing conflict is to ensure your team can fulfill their independent and interdependent roles. Having clarity of your role and embracing those responsibilities will go a long way toward preventing conflict.

Facilitate Thorough Communication

To prevent conflict, there is no substitute for thorough communication. Provide your team with a clear understanding of the connection between the work each does and how it ties to the work of others. When there is interference and a team member's work is affected, identify (ideally in a group setting) who else is impacted and who can help get things back on track. Allow your team to see how their work ties into that of others; it enhances their understanding of the power they wield and builds ownership for the work. Developing this clarity helps ensure your team can work fluidly—that each member remains accountable for their part and their impact on others.

Clearly defining roles and expectations, including the levels of interaction and group support that you deem essential, will prevent most conflicts, build your team's success, and enhance each member's joy in doing the work.

True, it is not possible to prevent all conflicts from occurring. Even among the most collaborative and cohesive teams, misunderstandings happen, feathers are ruffled, or pride gets in the way of acknowledging good work. But when a team lacks cohesion, the opportunities for conflict and tension increase exponentially. That's why your support of the collaborative activity on your team is of paramount importance.

Recognize Passion and Purpose (Can Ignite Tensions)

A final point worth noting is that tensions will rise more quickly among those who care deeply about the work. The more passionate they feel, the more committed they become, and potentially, the more frustrated they are when an obstacle stands in their way.

You undoubtedly want a team of passionate high achievers who care deeply about results. But that means you invite the potential for sparks of passion to occasionally fly. These dedicated professionals are your rock stars. You want them to stay eager and committed. Just as with any team member, you will prevent most conflicts by being available, listening when they voice concerns, and removing the hurdles that stand in their way.

When Prevention Doesn't Work, Don't Wait

While conflict prevention is the most desirable option, your efforts will be far from foolproof. Sadly, I have found most organizations lack a plan for managing more resilient tensions and unexpected spikes of conflict. Leaders trust that everything will be fine. Their *plan* is to deal with issues as they arise.

Without a clear plan, however, tensions have time to deepen or spread before actions take place. They grow from frustration to divisiveness. Left unresolved, workplace conflict can lead to a loss of talent and creates an unhealthy work environment. Some issues elevate to litigious actions or worse.

When working without a plan, each issue must be handled ad hoc, and only the escalated issues get attention. What lessons does that teach? What message does it send to your staff?

STRATEGIES FOR MANAGING CONFLICT

Because prevention has its limits, having strategies for managing conflict is essential. As the leader, your action (or inaction) sets the tone of employee interactions. To establish a healthy work environment where conflict is handled productively, you must take an active role.

Before I go on, let me clarify that conflict management and conflict resolution are not the same. Conflict management includes the efforts you make to slow or stop the progress of conflict. Conflict management addresses the conflict-inducing situation such as disagreements over the process of doing the work or friction over decision-making. It includes intervening at a stage when tensions, while climbing, are not critical. Conflict management contains the problem. By contrast, conflict resolution is used to resolve the issue between the affected parties. It is needed when emotions have become heightened and disruptive behavior is taking place. Conflict resolution becomes necessary when conflict management fails to identify or address growing concerns.

The strategies that follow will guide you in ensuring that conflict is managed thoughtfully and with an unbiased response.

CONFLICT MANAGEMENT BASICS

Principle #1 – Keep It Close

Conflict is most effectively managed at the level in which it occurs and therefore should always start there. Team members experiencing conflict will receive the most informed response from the manager or supervisor of their group. Peer support may also be successful. Taking an issue up the chain of command, to another department, or even HR, however, is not ideal. Those individuals, dedicated and interested though they might be, will be less informed about the individuals and circumstances surrounding the dispute. Any change they make could have unintended consequences.

Here are some considerations for conflict management planning:

- Provide training. Assigning responsibility won't work if vital skills are not developed. Those who manage others will need support in developing skills in communication, managing difficult conversations, and resolving conflict.

- Determine the circumstances for elevating an issue beyond the direct supervisor.

- Clarify who will be informed of the issues being addressed.

Principle #2 – Everyone Has a Role

Because conflict is best managed at the level in which it occurs, every supervisor, manager, and leader must clearly understand their role in managing conflict. They must know their responsibilities as well as the limitations of their involvement. It must be simple and straightforward enough to manage issues fairly, consistently, and appropriately.

Employees will need to know their role in bringing issues or concerns forward. They will need clarity about how an issue will be treated and what they can expect. They must be made to feel comfortable bringing their issues forward.

Finally, everyone in the organization must be committed to the same purpose: resolving conflict at the earliest stage possible.

These are some considerations for conflict management planning:

- Identify roles and responsibilities. For example, leaders, managers, and supervisors have a role in managing the conflict on their team; and each employee has a responsibility to speak up and seek help rather than acting out.

- Ensure that employees know when to access help and have clear guidance on whom to speak with.

- Ensure leaders, managers, and supervisors identify to their team *how* they would like to be informed of an issue or concern.

- Determine the information that will be kept confidential. Inform employees of these guidelines.

Principle #3 – It's Better with a Champion

With individual responsibilities spread throughout the organization, it is often essential to have a person focused and dedicated to this effort. Your champion will ensure that consistent efforts are made, and desired outcomes are achieved.

The champion will check in regularly with employees to determine if issues are being brought to the table. They will routinely meet with managers, supervisors, and other leaders to ensure those leaders are ready to support their teams and manage any rising conflict. The champion's role is that of a sounding board and problem-solver, helping others identify and process what needs to be done.

Determining the right champion differs from organization to organization but is often a VP of People or a leader in Human Resources. Already familiar with policies, interpersonal dynamics, and, we hope, holding a positive relationship with all employees, these professionals typically have both the reach, and breadth of knowledge and experience to be helpful.

Additional considerations for conflict management planning:

- Leading an initiative of this magnitude requires time and dedication. Employees will need to trust this person. Consider those best suited and most energized toward this purpose as you determine who will champion this cause.

- Identify a second person (champion) who can be called upon when your primary champion is unavailable or is seen as being biased on an issue.

Basic Principle #4 – Modeling Matters

Healthy conflict management starts at the top. As a leader, you must show your team that you are open, communicative, thoughtful, and transparent. If you have a champion, engaging with them and showing clear support for their role encourages others to do the same. As you demonstrate these positive behaviors, you give rise to teams that interact productively, and access their resources when necessary. While your behavior alone will not determine the outcome of a conflict, it can determine the willingness and flexibility of your team to come to the table and listen. As the leader, what you do matters. You are the starting point, the true north of acceptable behavior.

Consider these for conflict management planning:

- Identify ways to encourage employees (at all levels) to bring their concerns to the table.

- Acknowledge your managers and supervisors who are actively supporting their team through conflict management.

C.A.L.M. the Conflict

Managing conflict means staying in front of the issues, being ready to respond to them when they percolate to the surface, and supporting your team in resolving issues on their own. To do that, you must stay CALM.

The backbone for managing conflict, reducing tensions, and helping your team resolve their issues appropriately requires **C**onnection, **A**cknowledgment, **L**istening, and, only then, **M**anaging the conflict by taking action. I refer to this as the CALM approach.

Step 1 – **C**ONNECT (WITH YOUR TEAM)

Having a positive connection with your team is essential for managing conflict. Connection builds trust and confidence. It allows your employees to feel safe in sharing their concerns. When you have a strong connection with your team, you are poised to be aware of and therefore prepared to help address issues of conflict that emerge. Being connected also makes you more likely to notice those small changes in behavior which could denote that something is wrong.

For your employees, connection builds a feeling of being valued. Imagine that you have formed a strong professional connection with a member of your team; we'll call her Sally. Sally believes you value her work and see her contributions as necessary and important. Because she feels appreciated, when Sally has a workplace issue, she trusts her concerns will be met with your interest and support. For that reason, she openly shares these matters with you.

By contrast, consider a team member who does not experience a feeling of connection with you; we'll call him Beau. Missing that connection, Beau is less likely to feel valued by you and may doubt your willingness to aid or support him even for addressing the very same issues experienced by Sally. Rather than bringing the matter to your attention, Beau would be expected to withhold his concerns from you.

Staying connected in that way enhances your ability to learn about issues early on. With that awareness, you can address conflict as it emerges, and you can maintain far greater control of your team's ability to be collaborative and productive.

It is worth noting that your demonstration of support and willingness to help your team is more important than your competency for resolving their conflicts. Why? Because by being connected, you ensure that their conflict gets addressed even when you cannot directly resolve the dispute.

Leaders who have formed a solid and genuine connection with their team, where each member feels the leader recognizes their value and contribution to the whole, are well positioned to excel in managing conflict.

Step 2 – ACKNOWLEDGE (THE CONFLICT)

When tensions are brewing, the most essential step you can take is to verbally acknowledge the problem at hand. You may notice friction during a meeting or hear an offhand comment made by a member of your team or through the channels of gossip. However you become aware of the friction, and even when you only suspect its existence, acknowledging the conflict and sharing that recognition is your first step to bringing about change. Acknowledgment creates an opportunity to discuss the situation, modify the trajectory of the behaviors, and reduce or eliminate the underlying tensions.

Acknowledging the issue is not easy. Many leaders I have encountered cringe at this notion. They don't want to get involved; they don't want to know about the conflict or invite discussion about it. Some believe that doing so will give credence to the problem or make it worse. This is not the case. Avoiding or ignoring conflict is a tremendous mistake. It allows it to grow, fester, and spread.

To illustrate this and keep you from making this mistake, I'll describe a few of the most common avoidance strategies and the outcome of those efforts:

Feigning Ignorance

Many leaders wanting to stay out of the fray will feign ignorance to an issue. They may actively ignore a problem playing out right in front of them or turn a blind eye to challenges they know are occurring behind the scenes.

The primary issue with selective ignorance is that it provides a ripe opportunity for the conflict to grow and radiate. Without intervention, seeds of discontent quickly grow into adversarial relationships and toxic work environments. Conflict is like a weed. It grows and spreads, becoming ever more difficult to root out.

The secondary issue is that ignoring conflict impacts a leader's reputation. Disregarding an issue speaks to either the leader's ignorance about the problem or his lack of interest in resolving it. Neither is a good look for any leader. It sends a message that the team doesn't matter or that the leader lacks competence for managing others. That belief quickly stretches beyond those directly involved in any dispute. Others, who are undoubtedly aware of the issue, receive this message as well.

Finally, by feigning ignorance as a means of *staying out of it*, leaders lose a tremendous opportunity to let each team member know of their value. Instead, the assumption remains that the leader doesn't care, and those involved don't matter and aren't valued.

Minimizing the Problem

Leaders minimize conflict for a variety of reasons—because they are uncomfortable with conflict, they don't know what to do about it, they don't have the time or energy to deal with it, or they simply think the issue is insignificant and not worthy of their time or attention.

Leaders who minimize the conflict are prone to say things like "Let it go" or "Move on." I've known some leaders striving to be fair, to have said that to an entire team. Some promise, though neglect to, come back to the issue later. I've also known a leader to tell a member of his team to, "Put on your big boy pants and deal with it" rather than offering guidance or support. Actions like these don't address the issue. At best, these antics kick the proverbial can down the road, leaving the problem to be dealt with later. At worst, they add fuel to the already burning fire.

Unaware of the mistake of pushing past the issues, these leaders dismiss it. They view the conflict as an unnecessary hurdle. I've found some resent the team for bringing the issue forward. Others gaslight those who complain, blaming them for creating the problem. Rather than addressing the employee's concerns, these leaders direct those in crisis to push past it. In so doing, the leader is judging the importance of the issue. The leader's involvement, intentionally or not, serves to shame those experiencing or complaining about the conflict.

Beyond the damage of creating shame for those on the team is the reality that people can't simply let go or move off an issue because they are instructed to do so. The mere suggestion often creates resentment toward the leader or causes the person to double down in their beliefs or complaints. They seek to prove the leader wrong, to press that the issue *does* matter.

The Quick Fix

Many leaders' process for managing conflict is to provide a quick-fix solution. Their efforts include separating team members, switching someone's desk location, adjusting the reporting structure, or transferring a member to a different team or department. While they succeed in making things look different, the reality is that the leader has neglected to address the underlying issue. The issue commonly resurfaces in a new location.

The underlying problems often arise from struggles with communication, accountability, respect, or other behaviors we know as essential for a healthy, high-functioning team. A superficial change will not attend to those deeper problems. The "quick fix" further negates the potential positive result of showing the team they matter to the leader and, by proxy, the organization: that they are worthy of having their issue resolved. It also eliminates the possibility to learn (through the process of working it out) new skills for communicating and managing conflict. The quick fix costs the leader an opportunity to build and develop her team while very likely planting the seeds for further conflicts down the road.

Believing It Will Self-Correct

Finally, some leaders don't engage because they believe the employees will work it out on their own or that the problem will otherwise self-correct.

Leaders holding this viewpoint usually have a broader pattern of avoidance. In other words, their belief that the situation will self-correct is an extension of their justification for having ignored or minimized the issue. Unfortunately, regardless of the underlying reasons, this belief is misguided.

By the time an issue has reached a leader's awareness, it is rarely early in the development of conflict. More often, the conflict between individuals has been built on second, third, and fourth chances. It is the result of repeated disappointments and ongoing frustration. In fact, an issue won't often register as conflict, even among those directly involved, until an unacceptable pattern or trend has emerged. At that point, the problem is rarely settled with self-correction.

Instead, that is the point at which behaviors or complaints first start coming to light and reaching the awareness of others. It typically begins at the peer level, as team members complain, seek others with a shared viewpoint, or begin to make snarky comments. It takes time before the issue becomes large or significant enough to reach the leader's attention. By that point, the brewing tensions will not just go away. Therefore, it is incumbent upon the leader to acknowledge and address issues that reach their awareness.

There is a myriad of ways a leader can avoid team conflict. The priority, instead, should be *acknowledging* the conflict.

It's Not Only Leaders — Employees Do This Too

It's important to note that acknowledging conflict is not only a challenge for leaders. It is similarly common for those involved in such a situation to comparably ignore it, minimize it, and avoid it for as long as they can.

An employee may be embarrassed at being involved in a conflict. They may feel the issue is insignificant, will self-correct, or that it is beneath their leader to help resolve it. Similarly, an employee may hold back if they think being a party to an interpersonal struggle will reflect poorly on them. If they believe the employee with whom they are struggling is *favored* by the leader or organization, that too could hamper the process. There are endless reasons why an employee may withhold their concerns, especially early on. In fact, by the time you learn of it, problems may have been growing for weeks, months, or years.

That is why, as the leader, it is essential that *you* acknowledge the conflict. It allows your team to process through and address their issues or concerns. It gives them permission to accept their situation and to work toward resolving it. By acknowledging the issue, you can begin to control and change it.

Acknowledging the issue is a critical first step in managing conflict.

Step 3 – LISTENING

Once you become aware of a conflict, regardless of whether you believe you have the requisite skills for *resolving* the problem, it is your responsibility to manage that conflict. Your role is simple: listen. Listen to your team member who comes forward to discuss a concern and give them your undivided attention.

Listening is an essential skill, and there are dozens of books devoted to teaching and developing it. The core point is this; when it comes to conflict management, listening requires an intentional focus on the *perspective of others*. Before engaging in the more reflexive response of getting into helper mode and actively working to solve the problem, seek to learn the perspective of those making the complaint or bringing forward the issue.

Work to understand the point of view of those bringing an issue forward, even if you think it is obvious. Ask questions, learn why the situation is causing them problems and what they want to see changed. This may feel foreign to you or challenging as you want nothing more than to resolve the issue and move past the conflict. However, maintaining your focus on listening and learning is incredibly important. Avoid the temptation to solve the problem quickly.

You may be wondering, *Aren't some problems simple enough that I can just resolve them? Isn't it better to help my employee so that everyone can move on?* Maybe, but probably not.

Let me explain by way of an example. Say a member of your team, Juanita, comes to you and asks a seemingly straightforward question— one where you have experience and a ready answer. Juanita asks, perhaps rhetorically, "How am I supposed to work with Barry? He's impossible!"

Assume this is the first time you're hearing this from Juanita, but that you've worked with Barry in the past, and that is why the employee has come to you for counsel. If you get into helper mode, your reaction may be to commiserate and help the staff member feel better. Perhaps Barry is a pain to work with. Or, knowing this, you may offer Juanita solutions that you've found successful when working with Barry. You're trying to *resolve* the issue.

However, these seemingly helpful, innocuous responses have inherent flaws.

If, after hearing, "How do I work with Barry? He's impossible!" you begin commiserating or offering Juanita advice, you've effectively taken her side, validating her complaints about Barry. Consider the potential impacts of that. Juanita may now feel emboldened. She may feel you've got her back or agree with her. That, in and of itself, can cause things to spin in the wrong direction. But another circumstance may also occur: you've acknowledged that you know there is a problem working with Barry and that you have failed or are continuing to fail to address it.

Your quick *solution* has not helped anyone and may be placing your organization in legal jeopardy. Juanita now has the impression that the problem (Barry) isn't going away, that she will have to deal with him on her own. Barry has either been pigeonholed as a problem person, or he has been given a pass for his bad behavior. Finally, your role as the leader has been compromised as you aren't addressing the problem head-on. You may even have created a situation where Juanita now believes herself to be favored. The point here is that even minor issues require a more considered response.

Helping when you haven't begun by really listening can backfire. Your role is to listen until you truly understand the issue and the perspective of the person sharing their story. After that, you can begin to support the employee. In this example and in many situations, your support will entail coaching the person coming to you, guiding them so that they can solve their own problem. It follows the expression, "Give a man a fish; he'll eat for a day.

Teach a man to fish; he'll be fed for a lifetime."

When an employee like Juanita comes forward with an issue, your role is to ask questions, listen, learn about the situation, and gain the perspective of the person sharing their problem.

The questions I ask are purposeful and straightforward:

What is wrong?

Why is that a problem?

What is the impact?

How have you tried to resolve it?

What do you think will help?

These questions are *not* a simple checklist. Beyond the obvious, each has a specific purpose.

> *What is wrong?* This open-ended question invites a story. Depending on your relationship with the member of your team, they may keep this overly brief or use this single question as a way of answering not only this question but providing information on the

next two as well. If they keep their response overly succinct and you don't have all the answers, continue with the following question to gain the broader story. Your goal is to understand not only what is wrong but why they are coming to you.

Why is that a problem? You may think their answer will be obvious, but it often is not. I could tell countless stories of being surprised by the unique answers I hear. What you see as the problem may be far different than what the employee is experiencing. Even if you are correct, you demonstrate care and concern, good listening, and healthy leadership by discovering why the issue matters to *them*.

What is the impact? This question allows you to better understand "why" it is a problem. Again, even if it seems obvious, ask this question. The response will be invaluable in understanding the need and communicating it to others if necessary. The impact may be personal—it's causing stress, creating anxiety, or it may be related to their ability to be productive or maintain their reputation among their colleagues. All of these are valid and important. The impact informs you more specifically of why the issue needs addressing.

How have you tried to resolve it? Spoiler alert! Most often, people think they have tried when really, they've practiced patience and avoidance. These are not going to move the needle. Those efforts only suggest that the complaining employee believes the problem person is acting with malice or intent. Remember, vindicate; don't villainize. It is entirely possible that the problem person has no idea they are creating a problem. The complaining employee needs help to resolve the issue and the starting point is in learning what they have already attempted.

What do you think will help? Again, the answers may surprise you. Some employees don't know or just want to keep you informed. Some want drastic action. "Fire them." Others take pause and consider the question more fully. However they respond, it gives you guidance on the urgency of the matter and their vision for change.

After asking those questions and processing their responses, you will often find yourself in a position to coach the employee, allowing them to address the problem themselves. That is the role you will most often play—guiding and supporting others, enabling them to take necessary and appropriate action.

Step 4 – MANAGING THE SITUATION (TAKING ACTION)

Your final step for managing conflict on your team is to take action. However, your role is one of guiding not solving. You are helping your team learn to solve their problems. Returning to our example with Juanita and Barry, your role would be to provide your frustrated employee, Juanita, with guidance for communicating directly with Barry—to coach her with strategies for approaching Barry, sharing her concerns, and listening to his thoughts—to build her confidence to connect with Barry (vindicate not villainize) so they may jointly determine any necessary changes. That will allow Juanita the security of knowing you acknowledge her need for change and support her efforts to bring it about. Your wisdom is needed not your solutions. Your role is to identify the best strategies for engaging with Barry and provide a safety net if things don't go according to plan.

Your responsibility to your team is to contain the conflict, keep it from growing or spreading, and help those involved feel ready and able to resolve the issue for themselves.

But wouldn't it be so much faster if . . .

I know you're thinking it. You've probably jumped in and helped solve dozens of issues in the past. You may never have seen the problems that creates. It falls into your abyss.

Here's the reality. Attempting to shortcut this process—to offer solutions in lieu of connecting, acknowledging, and listening—will have consequences. Acting prematurely forces you to make assumptions about the situation. The assumptions alone will lead to frustration if you miss the mark. But more to the point, your haste suggests that the issue, and therefore those involved, are not worthy of your time. Each will cause them to feel disregarded, dismissed, or even betrayed. Even when your advice is sound, when you have not displayed CALM, your team may be hard-pressed to take it.

Once You're CALM, You Can Coach

Your role in managing conflict begins with understanding the needs of your team members. After you have acquired knowledge of the issue *as they see it*, your role transitions to coaching—coaching them to resolve the issue for themselves. Your role culminates with follow-up. Follow-up is essential as it verifies that the troubled employee has taken steps to address their problem and confirms that the necessary change(s) have occurred.

A Final Step – Follow Up

In keeping with our example of Barry, your follow-up would begin with Juanita, the frustrated employee. Your goal is to determine if the conversation she had with Barry was successful and led to both change and improvement. This final step is essential for confirming that progress is being made, or at least attempted. It would identify for you if Juanita successfully brought resolution to her issues.

By following up, you become aware when things hit a roadblock, the conflict is not resolved, or when additional efforts are needed. Common hurdles include that the troubled employee did not take action, is fearful or for other reasons resistant to bringing the issue directly to her colleague. The *bad Barry* refuses to engage or makes promises but does not change. It may even be that the conversation between Barry and Juanita went well, yet the problems persist.

Follow-up is essential for ensuring you remain aware of the progress in getting the issue resolved. If those involved have reached a workable solution, you can support them in following it. If they do not, you know that other steps or interventions are needed. Finally, and perhaps the most important reason to provide follow-up, is that it demonstrates to your employees that you value them and their role at the company.

STRATEGIES FOR RESOLVING CONFLICT

Sometimes issues are deeper rooted or further reaching than you first thought. Perhaps the team member (Juanita) who sought your counsel has made clear-cut efforts but has been unable to bring about change. Or, you have learned that the issues are not limited to her and have spread to affect the group or team. In those circumstances, providing support via one-to-one coaching will have limited success. The situation is most likely going to need a different level of involvement.

As an example, consider the case of *bad Barry* and presume you have learned that his behavior is so destructive as to be impacting the whole team. *Revisit the story about Stuart and Oliver for a real-life example of this situation.* In either circumstance, despite multiple members of the team making a concerted effort, no one has been able to bring about a shift or change. Your role as the leader is to attend to this issue directly to support the extended team, and in so doing, to ensure the wellbeing of the organization. As a leader, you have the authority and responsibility to do so.

Following are my guidelines for appropriately engaging in conflict resolution.

Listen to Both Sides

Conflict resolution, at its core, involves fairness and balance. When you are working to support a deeper issue, one where multiple people are involved, you must give equal time and weight to hearing the perspectives of each person or *side*. Ask questions to understand their needs, point of view, etc. Beyond the surface-level rationale of making things seem fair, gleaning the perspectives of all those involved is essential for identifying viable solutions.

You may be shocked to learn that I have conducted over 1,400 mediations during my career. In each mediation, I listen to the stories of the disputants one at a time. With few exceptions, the first story I hear is compelling. It seems to tell me everything I need to know. It guides me into seeing solutions for change.

Yet, my role is to hear both sides. So, while I may be tempted to move on to solutions, I wait and listen to the other side(s) to the story. And then it happens. I am surprised at what the second story reveals. It often alters my perspective completely as it transforms the whole situation. *This* shifting of view is the norm when resolving conflict. There is rarely a *bad guy* or unprovoked malintent underlying the problems. It is a matter of perspective.

To reach a legitimate solution, you must fully understand the problem. When you only hear one point of view, at best, you will only know half of the problem.

Vindicate; Don't Villainize

As you are listening to members of your team share their concerns, it is natural to feel drawn to one side of the story. While feeling that way is normal, acting on it is problematic.

In my work, I have maintained a firm belief that those at the heart of an issue, those seemingly responsible for the rising tensions or conflict, did not intend to create harm. I seek to understand the purpose or intention of their behavior. I look to vindicate not villainize them for their actions. This perspective allows me to stay curious not judgmental. As I hold that perspective, the person before me instinctively feels safe. They are willing to share their story. It becomes a positive self-fulfilling prophecy. I learn what is behind their behavior, and I can bring about change.

Maintaining that position will be of even greater importance for you. When you seek to vindicate not villainize, each team member will feel trusted and valued. Start by assuming each person involved in an issue has reasons that underlie their behavior. Approach them from a place of curiosity. Rather than guess the circumstances driving their conduct, probe with questions that help you understand it. It may be helpful to openly explain that you are trying to appreciate their perspective. When you engage your team like this, from a place of sincerity and with an open mind, you will find this process enlightening. People always have a reason for their behavior. Take the time to find out what it is, and you will see the path needed for change. And so might they.

Provide Transparency and Inclusion

When you support your team in working through an issue, transparency is essential. Openly share what efforts you will be making. Be inclusive and get feedback before enacting any changes. When you've listened to both sides of a story, resist the temptation to dictate an outcome. Rather, engage with those who will be impacted. Give them responsibility for identifying potential solutions. Allow them to determine what is needed. If giving that latitude is not possible and you must assume the role of the decision-maker, do it openly. Be honest about the reasons for addressing the issue yourself and what you expect as an outcome. Be inclusive, allowing all those impacted to hear what changes are happening and why.

Engage in Follow-Up

Conflict resolution is not the last step. Imagine you've engaged with those in conflict, and the issue has reached a conclusion. Areas for change and strategies for resolution have been negotiated and agreed upon. You, and those on your team, feel ready to move forward. However, don't be quick to assume the issue is behind you.

Change takes time, and no amount of effort ensures perfection. Even with a genuine commitment and dedicated effort, people will slip up, fall into old habits, or otherwise go back on their promises for change.

More to the point, a conflict that has come to your attention has no doubt been brewing for some time. Each employee's faith in the other's pledge for change is flimsy at best. As each extends their trust and offers false hope, they still expect to be let down. And, when human nature steps in and a mistake is made, it often seems that it was all for nothing. The impression becomes that the other party has not taken it seriously. That nothing has changed.

Your follow-up demonstrates your commitment to bringing forth meaningful change. It ensures that the process addresses the concerns and delivers the outcomes it intended to resolve. The follow-up process is similar to that used in other situations, but the approach is now more directive.

- Engage each involved party in a private conversation about the situation.

- Ask questions to determine the level of progress that has already taken place and identify what changes are still needed.

- Share that information with the other party. Where appropriate, highlight what each has done to honor the agreement (even if it didn't work out as planned).

- Discuss and clarify how they, you, or others can help bring about further needed change.

- Share next steps, including whom else you will be speaking with, when you will next circle back with an update or to check in on progress, and, where appropriate, alternative efforts that will occur to bring about change in the areas previously identified.

By staying engaged and following up, you can support the sanctity of the agreement that was reached. Your effort shows support for each person and a genuine desire to see a return to healthy workplace relations. Your follow-up effort will be instrumental in getting things back on track without inflaming the original conflict. If the agreement was flawed and left pieces unresolved, follow-up ensures that you are aware and can lead the team members in revisiting issues needing further attention.

Follow-up is key to success.

Putting It All in Action

To help you put the steps for conflict resolution in action, let's return to our scenario with Barry and Juanita. When we left off, you had coached Juanita. You had helped bolster her confidence and supported her in identifying ways to communicate her concerns and needs directly with Barry. Imagine now that the issues Juanita has been having with Barry have not improved and are increasing in frequency or intensity. Having already connected with Juanita, your next effort would be to engage with Barry (getting both sides). Your purpose is to alert Barry to the problem and then give him space to tell his side. That serves to identify his awareness of the issue, his perspective of the circumstances, and to explore his needs and concerns. Remember, no problem is ever one-sided. There are always important considerations for each person involved.

As you focus on vindicating Barry, he will be more likely to share the reasons for his actions or behavior. While hearing Barry's perspective may not affect the outcome or what ultimately needs to change, providing him with an opportunity to be heard will create a noticeable shift in his buy-in for the changes ahead.

For conflict resolution, this approach is both effective and necessary. *People want to feel heard and understood more than they want to be right.* Take the time to learn why a behavior is occurring. Seek to understand what underlies a lousy attitude. The outcome of your effort will go a long way toward resolving the problem and bringing about change.

Once the issues and perspectives have been heard and you have reached an understanding of what underlies Barry and Juanita's workplace struggles (for example, poor communication or weak boundaries), have Barry and Juanita determine solutions alongside you. Depending on the nature of the issue, you may be able to meet with them in a collaborative fashion (that's ideal), or you may do so with each separately. In either situation, ask them to share the concessions they will make to create productive change and resolve the issue(s). Do not work to create equality in the efforts each makes; instead, create balance in that each has a role to play in bringing about lasting change. In our example, Barry would likely have the lion's share of responsibility for bringing about change. But Juanita would be responsible for communicating with Barry about her needs and concerns in real time, helping Barry stay mindful of those needs.

Helping Barry and Juanita find a new normal for working together is not your last step. You will still need to circle back to determine if the changes are happening and working. Ask Juanita if things have changed? To what degree? Is there still progress? Does she feel things are better, or is further help needed? You would ask Barry similar questions about Juanita's efforts to improve the situation.

Where things have slipped up, your role is to help get them back on track. Encourage each to take ownership for any lapse and to recommit to the other their efforts to change.

Follow-up efforts are long-term efforts. Tensions and impressions are formed over time and will similarly take time to remove. Remain present and committed to the goal of having a healthy workforce. Remain a part of the solution by keeping your engagement strong. Your effort at managing conflict in this manner demonstrates your role as a leader and builds others' trust in you.

POINTS TO REMEMBER

Conflict management is a path not a destination. The process begins with taking steps toward prevention. Prevention is made possible by fostering trust, showing you care, openly committing to being helpful, modeling transparency and inclusion, ensuring team members understand both their role and that of others, and that boundaries between team members are upheld.

A leader who stays CALM can manage most issues of workplace conflict because they have formed a healthy relationship with their team. You can stay CALM by remaining connected, acknowledging the issues, listening, and, only then, managing the conflict situation.

As a leader, you are responsible for *supporting* your direct reports in resolving conflict not for resolving it for them.

To resolve conflict, listen to both sides, be transparent, and vindicate; don't villainize as you work to foster a resolution of the issues. Stay involved and committed to the efforts your team is making by keeping communication open and following up.

Quick Dos and Don'ts:

Don't

Ignore the conflict.

Minimize the conflict.

Make a judgment about the conflict.

Tell others to "move on" from the conflict.

Do

Acknowledge the issue exists.

Talk to *all* those involved.

Find out why the issue matters to them.

Find out what needs to change.

Be inclusive and transparent.

Stay involved—follow up.

CLOSING THOUGHTS ON FILL

FILL was designed to fill your bucket, offering you the opportunity to learn new skills and identify where, when, and why you will need to use them.

We began FILL by discussing the value of having true clarity about your role as a leader and identifying your three primary responsibilities:

- Identify goals.
- Set the direction of the team.
- Remove obstacles to success.

In FILLing your gap, I shared what creates obstacles for your team and how to remove them, as well as other strategies to prepare your team for success. You were introduced to the concept of an inverse organizational chart and were challenged to reframe your point of view about who supports whom in the chain of command. Finally, I provided direction for appropriately hitting the "Refresh button" should you recognize the need to shift your actions or notice that you and your team need a fresh start.

As we progressed into the section on trust, I shared the power of THOR You learned how trust and honesty differ and the intricacies of transparency, honesty, openness, and respect in building trust with others.

I provided an analogy about trust, comparing the challenge of reestablishing damaged trust to the experience of walking on thin ice. And here as well, I shared strategies for rebuilding and creating a fresh start when trust has been damaged.

Finally, in FILLing your gap in conflict management, I provided information and insight to help you prevent, manage, and resolve conflicts that erupt on your team. I taught you to remain CALM You learned why it is essential to have a conflict management plan, four basic principles of conflict management, and that a successful plan requires the involvement of every employee, regardless of level or role.

The FILL section tied together the importance of having solid trust and role clarity in your effort to manage conflict.

PART FIVE

OTHER LESSONS

more stuff you need to know
that no one is telling you

INTRODUCTION TO OTHER LESSONS

Even a good person with a kind heart and positive intentions will make mistakes, choose poorly, and cause harm. The point isn't to focus on blaming yourself; it's to focus on changing yourself.

The sections on FIND, FIX, and FILL have already left you feeling better prepared as a leader. You have learned what to do, what not to do (and why), and how to repair issues of trust, role clarity, and conflict management. But there is more to share to FILL your leadership gaps.

In Part Five, Other Lessons, I will cover some nuances of the information I already shared. In Chapter Twelve, you will learn what creates and destroys, accountability, and how to build that level of responsibility and dedication among your direct reports.

Moving into Chapter Thirteen, you will find detailed instructions for engaging in a difficult conversation. And while a difficult conversation is often best when held privately, you will learn ten reasons why you must sometimes move a corrective conversation into a group setting.

CHAPTER TWELVE

ACCOUNTABILITY

Business owners and high-level leaders often approach me with concerns about the future of their organizations. They speak to a lack of forward momentum or struggles in finding or retaining talent. But, more accurately, their concern stems from a fear that they lack future leaders. They feel stuck and without a growth or succession plan. How can they build the business, move on, or retire if they don't have capable hands in which to entrust the business? They boil it down to a problem with accountability.

This problem is not specifically one of succession planning. Many leaders see their direct reports as incapable or not trying hard enough. Where they want to see ownership and accountability, instead they see complacency.

The biggest problem with accountability is that leaders view the situation as stemming from the employee. They are quick to identify poor commitment, a lack of vision, or a failure to take ownership. As I'm about to show you, as a leader, you have more control over accountability than you realize.

ARE YOU UNDERMINING ACCOUNTABILITY?

Leaders who become frustrated when seeing a lack of initiative or momentum often step in to guide the work of one or more on their team. They push their employees to deliver the results they want to see. They are prone to micromanaging or dictating specific steps an employee must take.

Unfortunately, these strategies not only fail to bring the change the leader seeks, but they also create a self-fulfilling prophecy.

Legacy leaders are especially given to struggles with accountability, in no small part because they have a tremendous stake in ensuring the business's continued success. While their dedication seems positive on the surface, the energy and reaction it brings can be anything but. The story about Josephine's leadership speaks directly to this point. As a leader, Josephine's desire, perhaps even desperation, to leave the organization in capable hands and ready for continued growth caused her to step in. She was routinely involved, trying to guide or help.

While a leader's rationale for behaving in that way may be to teach next-level leaders the recipe for success, it instead narrows the opportunity for those next in line to be successful. It undermines their ability to display creativity, individuality, or problem-solving. The leader effectively limits the chance for their future leaders to perform at the expected level while also undermining those team members' passion and capacity to feel successful.

This phenomenon is not limited to legacy leaders. While some leaders are believed to interfere intentionally, not wanting their role or legacy to be eclipsed, most leaders legitimately want to see their team members succeed. And yet, their "helping" behaviors undermine that very objective.

There exists a delicate balance between setting your team members up for success and setting them up for failure. As I illustrate the common problems surrounding accountability, I'll explain why each situation creates interference and the strategies needed to bring change.

Problem #1 Limiting Responsibility or Control

As a leader, your team needs a degree of oversight. They seek your counsel. You want to be sure the work is done right. All of these are valid reasons you get involved. But there will be a backlash if your high-level engagement goes beyond the initial training period. Your involvement in your team's day-to-day work, your willingness to provide direct guidance, and your presence in the daily discourse all create a situation where your team members yield to you. When you represent yourself as knowing more or being better, you undermine your team's motivation and effort.

Whether these views are expressed overtly or subtly, the subliminal message is the same; you doubt your team member's ability, question their competency, or challenge their skill in making a good choice or decision. The overarching message is, "You're not good enough."

If your employee cares about the business and you as the leader, they may surrender to your message. That is especially true of long-term employees, those who've risen through the ranks, and those who deeply admire you as their leader. These employees may readily accept, or even adopt, your viewpoint. They don't want to let you down or disappoint you. So, they allow or invite the support. They ask you questions to prevent making a mistake. As a result, they don't learn or grow as needed. Their acceptance of the way things are generally appears as complacence.

In contrast, new hires, especially talented and self-assured additions to your team, are more likely to attempt to break free from your involvement in order to prove themselves worthy. If your behavior toward them remains the same as to longer-standing employees, it will undoubtedly create friction. They are trying to prove themselves, and you are standing in their way. For many, it leads to their departure. Those who are confident and talented will move on in search of a place where they can grow, prove their worth, and feel successful.

To shift the trajectory of your behavior, step back and stop comparing your team's work or skill to your own. If you believe they have more to learn, teach them. If you think they aren't the right fit, release them. The only way to be sure is to allow your team a much larger degree of control. When you do, look not just at what they deliver but at their level of satisfaction in the results they achieve.

To develop accountability, let them be their own critic and problem-solver. Success is rarely immediate. Developing skills and improving takes time. Rather than pre-judging what will or will not work, be a patient observer, encouraging behaviors that bring desired results.

Problem #2 Offering Poor or Incomplete Communication

As a leader, you may operate on a need-to-know basis or have access to privileged information. These situations lead to a level of under-communication. The lack of adequate information inevitably sets your team up for failure. They need to guess about priorities, the tie-in to the big picture, or the rationale for the work.

No doubt, some members of your team won't press you for information. They can't see or don't care about the big picture. Those are unquestionably the least valuable members of your team. They are worker bees and not ones from whom you can expect greatness or accountability. Like assembly-line workers, they do their job, shift the work process to the next person, and never ask or challenge the "why." Those employees may be necessary, but they are not your stars.

To build accountability, focus your effort on those who are seeking success. Those are the staff who press for information, ask good questions, and want to know *why*. They are more capable and interested in being contributors. Their curiosity indicates their ability to process, consider, or develop the information they receive. To build their success and your own, err toward offering more information than they may need, never less. Invite their questions and make time to answer them. When information is privileged, share what you can, and explain where you are limited and why.

When you openly share information, you demonstrate trust in your team. You are also modeling what you expect from them and building reciprocity of trust with them. In turn, it leads your team to openly share information (beyond the "need to know") with you. With that level of communication and transparency, you will become aware of potential problems and be able to get in front of them. You can also expect your team to be accountable for their performance, good or bad, because they have the information needed to succeed.

Problem #3 Setting Unrealistic Expectations of Success

Your team wants to do well. They want to succeed. Some may even want to shine for you. But if you create an expectation beyond their reach, they may feel defeated before they ever try. To be accountable for the result, expectations of success must be within reach.

While you steer clear of micromanagement, your role as a leader can include breaking down sizeable goals into manageable pieces, identifying benchmarks, and identifying a path for reaching milestones. Before establishing the objectives, engage with your team to ensure they have the knowledge, skills, and access to information that they need. Confirm that they understand their role, the purpose behind the effort or goal, and what success will look like. When you expect results without providing guidance, clarity, and information, your team cannot be responsible for the outcomes. They are unable to demonstrate accountability.

Creating accountability is almost always within a leader's control.

A leader who engages in micromanagement offers poor or incomplete communication or sets unrealistic expectations of success will set their team up for failure. By contrast, sharing information, giving opportunities, and allowing your team the room to stretch, fail, and learn from their mistakes sets them up for success.

Accountability Is Coveted Cultivated by Leaders

To be successful and reach your heights as a leader, one of your primary roles must be to develop the accountability of those on your team. While it is a quality coveted by leaders, cultivating accountability from each member of the group is their responsibility. That includes an individual's accountability for performing at the level you need and the team's accountability to collectively work and support each other for reaching their interdependent goals.

Your process to date has no doubt included identifying expectations and then stepping back, leaving room for your team members to strive to reach the goals you set. You hope and expect them to rise to the occasion, reach the goal, and prove their worth and value. That seems like a reasonable process and a fair expectation. After all, that is what you hired them to do. But that process will rarely lead to the results you desire unless you've taken other steps to prepare your team to be accountable.

Individual accountability comes as a byproduct of desire combined with competence and is rounded out with opportunity and self-confidence. As a leader, you can influence all four.

Consider your new hires. They come in enthusiastic, full of promise. You hired them because they exude passion for the work, and you believe they will be capable of performing well. Yet soon after coming on board, it seems they are failing you. They stagnate. They aren't the person you thought you'd hired. In all likelihood, you wonder what went wrong.

Most likely, it wasn't poor hiring. Instead, you probably neglected to develop your employee's level of accountability. You've missed a step in preparing them to be successful in your organization and under your leadership.

Let me illustrate by sharing a story from my work history. It isn't purely a story of accountability but of learning. In 2000, I was hired to lead a peer mediation program in two Santa Monica, California, middle schools. The dispute resolution agency that hired me offered me the role because of my credentials, background with youth, and newfound passion for mediation. I was given the part of running this school-based program just six weeks after completing my own initial training in mediation.

One of my first responsibilities was to recruit and train the student mediators. My boss, Deborah, introduced me on the campuses, gave me basic directions for how many students to bring on and train at each school, and provided me with a training outline.

The recruitment and selection phase needed to be done quickly so that the program could quickly be up and running. I had about three weeks to select thirty kids per school. Immediately following that, I was to lead a three-day off-campus training. My role for the program involved everything from logistical planning to supplying food and drinks to providing the twenty-one hours of training to sixty middle school students.

And then the training began just two months from my date of hire and three months from when I'd become a mediator myself. I was the only trainer. I was in one large room at a community center with the objective of training sixty middle-schoolers in peer mediation over three days. I soon learned that the curriculum provided to me was grossly inadequate. Day one was a disaster.

The materials were lacking in exercises. The kids took excessive trips to the bathroom and used breaks to run around the community center. Some started roughhousing, and one kid nearly broke his arm. Days two and three were modestly better as I spent the night before each developing materials and worksheets that I could use to further their learning and engagement. But I couldn't wait for it to be over.

Deborah had let me know that this process would need to be repeated in the spring semester. More student recruiting, more training. I liked and respected Deborah. In truth, she became my mentor, and we enjoyed a great friendship over the years. But that day, still new to the job, I told her no. I agreed to conduct the spring program but told her that in the future, the training program would occur only in the spring. I would instead have the prior year's trainees participate in a refresher training in the fall, thereby remaining active for the following year. Deborah allowed the pushback and let me determine the future course of the program.

In the spring, I led the program the second time as requested. In between, I developed a full curriculum and a training workbook for the three-day program. I determined better logistics, including laminated bathroom passes, limiting the number of water bottles each student could have, and pre-teaching the students about my expectations.

At the end of the three-day session, a community center member was helping me load up my car with the remaining supplies. He complimented me on how well I ran the program and how well-behaved the kids were. Then he began to tell me a story about the last person who'd run the program for the agency and what a mess it had been. He was talking about me.

I listened for a few moments, then interrupted to tell him he was talking about me. I expected him to laugh and stop.

Instead, he waved me off, apparently thinking this to be impossible. After all, it was just a few months prior.

I stopped him again, sharing some of the chaos that had transpired and again saying, "That was me."

His eyes got huge.

I explained that I had not been prepared and didn't know what to expect but that I learned quickly and addressed the problems. The lesson is simple: when you give people a chance to learn and grow, they are likely to rise to the occasion.

I ran that program for seven years. I became the leader of the youth program within just a few months. And that curriculum I developed is still being used today, over twenty years later.

Deborah was far more seasoned than I was in mediation, program administration, and leadership. I liked and trusted her. However, had she decided to help "fix" the wrong things or dictate how I was to do my job, I would not have been free to create what ultimately was a success—for myself, the organization, and the youth we supported.

Looking back, I see that it was Deborah's willingness to trust me that built my accountability. It also increased my ownership of the work and my passion for further building up the program.

DEVELOPING ACCOUNTABILITY IN YOUR TEAM

While not every employee will be as awesome as I was (smile), every leader can foster the accountability of those on their team by building on their team members' desire and sense of competency, providing opportunities, and bolstering the confidence of their team as they try new things.

Desire

To build accountability, start with desire. An individual's desire is a key factor in their *interest* in being accountable. Their desire is connected to their pride in their role and in the company. You got a glimmer of that during the hiring process, but that glimmer cannot sustain itself. You must fan the flames of desire, building and supporting it with your direct reports. It's not complicated. It involves sharing *your* passion and enthusiasm.

Build on your team's desire by sharing the purpose of the work. Help them develop a connection to it. Why does the work matter? What will it build toward? How does their work support that effort? How does it all fit into the bigger organizational purpose?

Ideally, you begin building their desire on day one, during the onboarding stage. There, each employee is just learning about the organization and their role within it. You can bolster that desire by engaging the employee in a discussion about the business, then tying it directly to the work they are performing. Desire connects to motivation. Motivation lends itself to accountability.

Competence

You influence an employee's future accountability based on how you develop or destroy their feelings of competency. Unless an employee is delusional, and yes, there will be some who fit that profile, a team member's feeling of competence is related to their performance and the feedback they get for their work. What message do you provide your team to tell them they did well? Do you tend toward finding fault or seeing success? Do you tell them what they could do better or inquire about what they would do differently next time? How do you treat them when they do well or poorly on a task or project? The way you manage performance will dictate your team members' feelings of competence. It will determine whether they try hard to please you or stop caring about the results.

To build their sense of competency, ask questions to better understand their view of the situation and what might need to change. Encourage them to stretch when they demonstrate growth and learning. Support them with mentoring and opportunities to learn more.

Opportunity

Providing direct reports—especially next-level leaders—with opportunities to stretch and contribute beyond their current level builds future accountability. Where this goes awry is when the opportunity is saddled with micromanagement or diluted by having too many others involved. Accountability requires a degree of self-governance and focuses heavily on self-reliance. Providing a team member with the opportunity to have sole responsibility for something promotes thinking things through, inspires learning, and encourages ownership.

How you offer this opportunity has an impact as well. Do you make it safe for your team to pursue such an opportunity, or is it linked to a threat of repercussion if things don't go well? Do you build their confidence that success is within their reach or challenge them to perform in a way that is likely to lead to failure? Your actions determine if the opportunity you present is one worth pursuing.

Self-Confidence

Lastly, to support accountability, be sure your team member has a reasonable degree of self-confidence. To develop self-confidence, foster your team members' belief in themselves and their skills. This connects to the opportunities you afford them. As you assess if they are progressing and gaining new skills, also examine how their desire and competence come together when they encounter a hurdle or make a devastating mistake. The self-confident team member, ready to take on greater responsibility while demonstrating accountability for the results, is willing to own their mistakes, learn from them, and display competency toward making better choices in the future.

When you build up a team member's self-confidence, you build their buy-in. It will bolster not only their capacity to be accountable but their desire for it. It creates a cyclical event.

To enhance the self-confidence of a member of your team, consider this: do you praise hard work and effort? Do you encourage staff to think things through, giving opportunities to rethink a response if you present them with an issue they had not considered? Or are you prone to criticize mistakes or failures to accomplish goals? How *you* look at mistakes or failures—as catastrophic or as opportunities for growth and learning— plays a large part in how confident your team will feel.

Developing a team rife with accountability is possible. While you can't force desire, you can inspire it. Where you can't create competency, you can teach and build toward it. You determine the level of opportunity you afford your team so that they stretch themselves and grow. Your response to their efforts can support or hinder their confidence, thereby impacting their willingness to try again.

Developing accountability on your team is yours to control, and it is most definitely within reach.

POINTS TO REMEMBER

A leader's actions determine the accountability of those on their team. While not every employee is the right 'fit' for their role, it is the leader who controls the level of accountability that their team ultimately demonstrates.

A leader will develop accountability on their team by:

- Helping each employee feel connected to the work they perform.
- Acknowledging good performance and providing helpful and timely feedback.
- Providing opportunities for employees to stretch themselves.
- Fostering self-confidence by recognizing mistakes as normal and critical to learning.

ACCOUNTABILITY DOS AND DON'TS

Don't

- Limit responsibility or control of your employees
- Offer poor or incomplete communication to those on your team
- Set unrealistic expectations of success

Do

- Help employees through teaching; then allow them a chance to try again.
- Give employees control over the results of their actions.
- Offer more information, not less. Invite questions. Give context and details.

CHAPTER THIRTEEN

CRITICAL CONVERSATIONS

Each story in this book illustrates an issue or series of issues that mark the missteps made by leaders and the fallout it brought to those on the team.

While I have explained the fundamental issues of trust, role clarity, and conflict management and provided clear guidance on how to FIX and FILL those gaps, there is an essential skill I have not yet covered: *how to have a difficult conversation.* This skill is often the missing link between knowing what to do and how to do it. You can have endless knowledge about how to lead, but without the ability to have critical conversations, you and your team will suffer.

A difficult conversation is one that is expected to be uncomfortable for at least one of the people involved. For that reason, many people avoid having it. Yet, it is the avoidance of engaging in a difficult conversation that causes things to go awry—when a problem that should have been easy to address begins to fester, grow, and create damage.

What amounts to a challenging conversation for you will vary. It may relate to giving feedback, addressing problem behavior, or telling someone they've hurt you. *Note: The technique I'm about to share is also effective in personal conversations.*

Regardless of what makes a conversation feel difficult, the process I'm about to teach you works because it never lays blame or challenges the other person for their behavior. Instead, it looks for acknowledgment of the problem and then explains why change is needed. This process focuses on building awareness and empowering the other person to devise *their* plan for change. And it holds them accountable.

Before I go through the step-by-step process, let me acknowledge that you may feel resistant to having a difficult conversation. If so, you may be forgetting one of the basics: vindicate not villainize. Rather than imagining the person you are about to speak with has been engaging in their behavior with willful intent to create harm, reframe your mindset. Vindicate; don't villainize. Approach them with the belief that they are not yet aware of the impact they are having or why they need to act differently. Reframe your mindset. Consider that you are offering them a gift by sharing information they will need to succeed.

ENGAGING IN A DIFFICULT CONVERSATION

Let's get down to basics. Engaging in a difficult conversation requires preparation. The easiest way to control how your message is received will be to plan for the proper delivery. Time and place are as important to consider as the topics you intend to broach.

Preparation

1. Plan for the conversation to be held privately and professionally. A difficult conversation deserves focused attention, not a drive-by attack. Similarly, do not engage in a difficult conversation over a shared meal or while driving in a car. The person you are speaking with should feel they can remove themselves from the situation at any point if they so choose. Your selection of time and place should create a feeling of safety while also demonstrating importance.

2. Make an appointment with the person and give them the gist of what you want to talk about. As an example, you might say, "Bob, I'd like to talk to you about your project that's behind schedule. When do you have time to meet this week?" This allows Bob to be in the right mental state when you sit down to meet, and it keeps him (and you) from being caught off guard by an impromptu discussion.

3. Schedule time for the discussion that is *longer* than you believe you will need. The minimum amount of time you should schedule for such a conversation is thirty minutes. Often, an hour is more appropriate.

   The time frame ensures that both you and the person with whom you are speaking know that there is gravity to the discussion. You are committing time to it, which in and of itself speaks to the importance you place in the matter.

   Further, the point of a difficult conversation is that it is indeed a conversation. It is a two-way dialogue where each takes time to listen, explain, understand, and draw conclusions. None of that is possible in a rushed conversation. The added time allows you to discuss the issue, create a plan for change, and determine how follow-up will occur.

4. Be clear about what you want to discuss, remembering your goal is to build awareness not criticize. I suggest that you prepare for your meeting with the following:

   • The facts about the problem you want to discuss. In other words, what exactly has happened to bring about this conversation.

   • The negative impact of the situation on the person you are speaking with and the organization as a whole. (Do not make the issue about other people). Here, you are explaining why this situation matters.

   • Your thoughts for a solution. These should be proactive measures— things the person can begin to do. It is the how and identifies what they can do, rather than focusing on what they must stop doing.

During the Meeting

1. Once the meeting begins, engage in a brief exchange of niceties before getting down to business. This may be something like, "Thanks for taking the time to meet today, Bob. I know you have a lot on your plate, so let's get down to business. I want to tell you why I've called you in here."

   The longer you wait, the more niceties you exchange, the more uncomfortable the situation becomes, and the less time you leave for addressing the issue at hand. Get to it quickly.

2. Next, state the facts. This should be a short story or description that explains the problematic situation.

3. Wait for their response.

Remember, I said this would be a conversation. It is, right from the beginning. In giving difficult news, you should expect a response from the listener. Welcome it. Ask for it. Pause for it. Until the other person responds, you won't know if the message was understood or accepted.

Of note: It is expected, even helpful when the person attempts to defend themselves. It means they care about their reputation. They feel frustrated and want relief. They want you to understand them and their perspective. These all help identify the information needed to reach a positive conclusion. But we're not there yet.

4. After they finish, genuinely thank them for their response, as appropriate, acknowledging that their comments have added to your perspective. Do *not* engage in a discussion about their specific comments.

In most circumstances, what they share changes nothing about what you need to discuss. It just brings new details about the problem. However, listening and expressing gratitude for their sharing builds their willingness to listen and engage with you.

5. It's your turn again. After thanking the other person, redirect the conversation back to your *why*. Restate the basic premise of the problem (the *what*) and then continue the thought by expressing how that is negatively impacting the organization *and* how it is negatively impacting them.

This is the aha moment for the person in front of you. You are helping them see why the problem you shared is a problem for them. But, because it is affecting them, you must include the big-picture impact as well.

6. Ask them if they have any suggestions or solutions that might help improve the situation.

Wait for them to come up with some. Allow them to waffle for a bit as they consider your offer of determining the result for themselves.

7. Once they have listened to their ideas, good or bad, offer to share your own. *Offer* is the operative word. You want them to actively agree to hear your suggestions. This primes them to listen and consider them. Note: *Your ideas were the third thing you had prepared before the meeting.*

Often at this juncture, there is a bit of negotiation and discussion of options and strategies.

8. As the conversation continues, you will want to firm up the commitments for change.

I suggest you agree that the terms of the discussion will be put in writing and sent via email as a way of keeping clear on the agreements that you each have made.

Your part of the agreement, at a minimum, will be to keep tabs on the situation and to check in regularly to provide support or guidance as needed.

9. Close the meeting by thanking the person for having met with you and taking the time to create a plan for change.

After the Meeting

Follow up. This solidifies the importance of the initial conversation and the changes that were deemed necessary.

Within a short but reasonable period, check in with the person you have met with. Depending on what is happening, you will respond in one of the following ways:

1. Change is happening, and it's great.

Checking in confirms that you noticed their effort and satisfies them that it mattered enough for you to pay attention.

Speak to the results that their change is creating. Credit their effort or give a genuine compliment. It is a great way to encourage them to keep it up.

2. Only moderate change has occurred.

If they are trying but not entirely successful, compliment their effort while opening communication about other steps they can take. This may lead to another discussion about solutions.

3. Change is not happening.

Checking in when change is not happening shows that the original issue was significant and continues to be important.

Focus on the lack of change and the need to readdress it. Typically, this means renegotiating the solutions. But it may also lead to a conversation about consequences.

Follow-up is not a one-and-done event. It occurs frequently and repeatedly until you see successful change. Then it continues, but with diminishing frequency, until the new behaviors are fully integrated and routine. It is still a good practice to offer an occasional acknowledgment of the effort and the reasons it was successful.

To get a free downloadable of this process, go to CandiceGottliebClark.com/FindFixFill

If you're curious to see how this process works in an actual situation, I've taken two of the stories from this book to illustrate the process of engaging in a difficult conversation. These examples are also found by going to CandiceGottliebClark.com/FindFixFill.

MAKING THE CONVERSATION PUBLIC

Most critical conversations are held privately. That serves to protect the person on the receiving end from any embarrassment while encouraging the dialogue that is essential for bringing about buy-in and change.

However, there are times when a private conversation does not bring about the desired change. That was true in the story about Stuart. Stuart had spoken to Oliver about the issues (though not using the model described above), but no noticeable change occurred, and the impact on the team was growing. Stuart needed to make the conversation—and his efforts—more public.

So when, why, and how does the conversation leave the private realm?

When you've sought to address an issue privately, but no change has been observed, and your team continues to be impacted by the behavior (and is therefore awaiting change), it is time to adjust your strategy for managing the situation that is creating conflict or tension. At that point, you must address the issue(s) among the team members—particularly those who are impacted.

Your effort to open the communication is not made to throw your problem person under the bus, embarrass, or discourage him. It is to open a dialogue among the team members that can bring about change. The only "side" you are taking is cohesion. Your goal is to help your team function fluidly without your direct involvement or need to referee.

Ten Reasons for Managing An Individual Issue In A Team Format

1. It validates your team. It shows that you acknowledge the problem they are experiencing and believe that change is important.

2. It allows the team to take ownership of the issue and why it matters. When you take yourself out of the middle, the team can share information about their concerns directly.

3. The team can provide context about the impact or disturbance for the person creating a problem. It would be a mistake for you to take this role, as it could be perceived as side-taking or favoritism.

4. The person creating the disturbance is given the opportunity to explain his actions or defend himself. *You* are unable to share those details on behalf of the problem person. To do so would involve playing middleman, and sharing those viewpoints would be perceived as side-taking. Your team member must defend *himself*. The difference in this public situation is that you are present to create safety and stability in the discussion.

5. You demonstrate support for the team in getting their needs met and the issue resolved. Your engagement and neutrality support everyone.

6. Your efforts establish that you value each member of the team and the contribution they are making or are trying to make.

7. Your team will bear witness to your efforts to resolve the issue. That isn't passing the buck; it is demonstrating the importance of bringing change and resolution.

8. You can provide a safe, constructive environment for discussion and resolution. By fostering a collective discussion, your focus can be on ensuring the team develops clarity and understanding—that their efforts lead to commitments and change.

9. You model the importance of healthy conflict communication. You demonstrate the ability to talk through issues that induce tension but are also catalysts of change and growth.

10. The inclusive approach means all parties are clear on expectations of change, and you can discuss your efforts to uphold the decisions made.

If you are not yet sold on the importance of transitioning to a public (team-oriented) discussion of the unresolved issue, please reread the last ten reasons until you are. It's critical to the health of your team and securing your role as the leader.

Rather than doubting the need to shift from a private to group forum, I hope the question you are asking yourself is, "How do I make this transition?" The "how" is incredibly important. You want to ensure your efforts build cooperation and bring change—that your team, including the problem person, feels supported, safe, and able to express themselves and their needs.

SETTING THE TEAM UP FOR A SUCCESSFUL RESOLUTION OF THE ISSUES

When you notice it's necessary to shift into a group format, begin by speaking to the problem person. Inform them of the concerns you (and the team) still have regarding their ability to work collaboratively. Let them know that you've decided a group discussion is essential, and then add in the relevant reasons (#3 and #4) from above. Get them on board by reminding them that in a group setting, the team can provide context about the issue and that they, in turn, will be able to explain their situation more fully to the team.

Next, approach the team (including the problem person) in a straightforward manner. A group email may be your best choice for communicating with the team, as it assures consistency in the messaging and reduces any concerns about side-taking or back-channel conversations. Let those involved know that you support them and want to ensure they resolve the issues by providing better transparency and open communication. In this message, provide them with essential details about when and where the meeting will take place, and confirm if the meeting is mandatory for them to attend (it is). Everyone on the team is impacted by the problem, and each must support the change. Therefore, everyone must attend.

Once you initiate the meeting, engage the team much as you would an individual in a difficult conversation. Engage them with a brief greeting, then cut to the chase of why you are all meeting. Share your expectations for the session. They should include the following:

- Building a better understanding of the issues
- Exploring options for change
- Determining solutions

You may need to ease the team into the session by sharing your efforts to date, or if you know they are ready to jump in, simply set parameters on how you'd like them to communicate during the meeting. Basic parameters should include rules for listening, taking turns, and asking questions rather than jumping to conclusions. Point out that getting sidetracked into the minutiae of day-to-day work is likely, so inform the team that for this meeting, you expect them to stay on task and focused on resolving the main issues or concerns.

If you believe this meeting will be overtly confrontational or you fear that you could lose control of the situation, call in a conflict resolution professional to support you and the team. Regardless of the cost, this is a small investment compared to the damage of creating dissolution of the whole team. As a reminder, this is what befell Stuart.

Taking action to hold critical conversations, be they held privately or in a group setting, is an essential part of your role. In doing so, you are managing conflict, and you are building trust. You're building accountability toward change and proving yourself to be an awakened leader.

A caveat about this team-oriented approach is that there are times when you will need to return the conversation back to a private one. A prime example for this might be if you determine disciplinary action is required. Once you recognize a need to engage in a level of discipline, the conversation between you and that team member must return to a private discussion. Depending on the severity of the behavior, you may table it until after the team meeting concludes, or it may be the catalyst for closing the meeting early. Regardless, your tone and engagement must remain professional and respectful. Even if the team is upset with their colleague, seeing a team member taken to task in a public setting will build concern among the team that their mistakes could be handled in a similarly gruff or public environment. This will impact their feelings of safety and trust.

Critical conversations are those that need to occur but seem difficult or highly uncomfortable. As the leader, you are responsible for engaging your team in these conversations—making them aware of the impact of their actions or decision-making.

POINTS TO REMEMBER

- Your role as the leader is to address the issue in support of the team.
- Problem behaviors are rarely an act of malice, nor do they commonly reflect a willful attempt to create harm.
- Vindicate not villainize as you seek to identify the underlying cause of the problem.
- Use the steps furnished for preparing, leading, concluding, and providing oversight and follow-up for the difficult discussion.
- When change does not occur, the difficult conversation needs to leave the private realm and include the entire team.

CHAPTER FOURTEEN

GETTING HELP
AND INVOLVING OTHERS

Your toolbox is now filled with knowledge and tools to lead your team successfully. You understand the three pillars for self-aware leadership: trust, role clarity, conflict management. You've learned the value of THOR for creating trust and how to manage conflict by staying CALM You recognize how your best intentions are not always enough, and you have a plan in place to address issues of trust, role clarity, and conflict management on your team.

As you show progress in implementing these techniques, you may still encounter issues you cannot resolve—issues such as persistent conflict or friction among your team. Team conflict is a lagging indicator of problems in trust, role clarity, and conflict management. While you may be taking steps to address these, the conflict that has begun will not simply evaporate. It will need to be resolved.

When conflict persists despite your efforts to resolve it or when it has gone beyond the scope of your comfort or skills, it is critical that you access alternate support before more damage occurs.

Directing team members to "get over it" or "move on" only brings other, more significant problems.

A substantial part of your role as a leader is to remove barriers to success. Conflict is a tremendous barrier.

OPTIONS FOR SUPPORT

When you cannot fully attend to the issues or ensure their resolution, your two options are internal support (often your Human Resource team) or external support (a conflict resolution professional). You may consider your Human Resource team your best advocate and the most appropriate place to turn for support. But I caution you against that.

While I hold Human Resource professionals in very high regard, I do not recommend you give them the responsibility for resolving internal or team conflicts. The reasons for this are related more to proximity than competency. Following are key issues that impact the success of an HR team in resolving conflict:

Limited Skills

While your HR team has a vested interest in supporting you and your team, have they been trained in conflict resolution? Mediation is a process, not a concept. If your HR person is not well versed in the art and skill of managing interpersonal conflict, this is not the time to learn. Managing conflict poorly or partially will make things worse.

Competing Duties

Resolving conflict requires dedicated and uninterrupted time and focus. The process cannot be rushed or done piecemeal if it is to be effective. Yet your HR team has many other tasks that require their time and attention. Their plate is typically overflowing with everything from employee benefits to recruitment and onboarding. They are also involved in monitoring employee performance and managing matters requiring discipline.

Trust Issues

The involvement of your internal HR team, as professional as they may be, is likely to create fear or concern. Given HR's access to employee records, they are presumed to have a jaded perspective on the issue. Further, HR has connections and possibly friendships throughout the company.

Using an internal resource will come with a degree of suspicion about confidentiality and potential repercussions. Without trust, your team will undoubtedly limit their sharing and engagement. They will withhold information that may be essential for resolution.

You Also Need a Safe Resource

As I said at the start of this book, leaders make mistakes. They don't know what they don't know. As such, it is quite possible the conflict—or at least its unrelenting growth—stems back to you. Who would you want informing you of this? Can you be sure HR is capable and comfortable giving you a hard truth? Finally, connecting back to the competency question, an HR leader may not be able to trace issues back to their source. You need someone who can resolve the immediate problems, find its source, and enlighten everyone about what needs to change.

THE ROLE OF HR IN CONFLICT MANAGEMENT

While your HR team is not appropriate for resolving internal issues of conflict, keeping them informed and engaged is hugely important.

- Members of HR can advise you about the connected aspects of managing conflict resolution, including the potential for progressive discipline or performance management.

- The department often has established connections and resources, which may include a workplace relations or conflict resolution expert. This will save you valuable time in getting the process of resolution quickly underway.

- Your HR team needs to be informed so that they can prepare for changes underway, including the potential for turnover.

- Your HR team may have information critical for steering you and the organization clear of legal issues.

- Finally, and perhaps most importantly, HR is a part of the leadership team and the hub for employee management needs. As the center point of all employees, HR may notice organization-wide trends and be quick to identify issues affecting other departments or teams.

Keeping them in the loop allows your Human Resources team to maintain responsibility for their role, allowing them to determine if strategic or company-wide efforts are needed.

THE ROLE OF AN EXTERNAL CONSULTANT

In contrast to HR, an external consultant arrives with a much higher degree of objectivity and an unclouded perspective of the conflict and the people involved. While you will undoubtedly debrief this consultant on the problem and the players, any specialist in conflict management will take that information with a grain of salt. (Yes, it's true.)

A good conflict resolution consultant will listen and glean *your version* or understanding of the problem. Then they will set about working with the participants in an unbiased manner. Someone in HR is rarely capable of doing so.

An external specialist is neutral to the issue. There is no history or bias developed—no friendships or relationships to influence their perception of the situation or the people. More to the point, any shame, embarrassment, or fear the employee may feel in connection with their dispute can be managed. The external resource hearing all the sordid details will not be a permanent part of the landscape. They won't be working down the hall or socializing with the employee's coworkers. Confidentiality, and therefore trust, are present.

An internal resource, HR or otherwise, will always be met with doubt. The fullness of their commitment to keeping things confidential will always be in question. The fears of your employees are grounded in reality. I have known more than a few HR leaders who made the unfortunate mistake of gossiping about a situation or who used the power of their knowledge as a warning, threatening staff to behave. Even if your internal Human Resources staff is above reproach, the trust cannot match that of bringing in an unbiased, neutral, outside provider.

FINANCIAL CONSIDERATIONS

Time and money are probably the most significant considerations leaders make when considering the use of an outside resource. Most leaders recognize that the work will take time away from their team's other responsibilities. Further, it costs money they didn't budget for. That may sound like a lose-lose.

If that is your concern, you're missing the big picture. Bringing in an outside specialist will actually save you both. Yes, there will be a time commitment and a financial investment. But you are also halting the damage and unwinding it. When conflicts are resolved, your teams work well together (better productivity), and no one is looking for their next job (talent retention). Unwanted turnover or further bleeding due to issues of conflict costs you far more in terms of time and money.

As an added benefit, your team members will know you are investing in them. That tells the team you value them enough to make that commitment. It demonstrates that you take their situation seriously and care that it gets resolved.

Conflict can undermine any leader. When it is disrupting your team, time is of the essence for getting things back on track. Your effort in addressing these issues underscores your competency as a leader. It demonstrates your strong role clarity as you remove barriers to the team's success. It illustrates your attention to conflict management. And it builds your team's trust in you as their leader.

POINTS TO REMEMBER

- Human Resource professionals are not positioned to be successful in managing internal conflicts. Competing duties and issues of trust are among the reasons they falter in this effort.

- Human Resource professionals should be kept involved and in the loop. They can provide valuable resources and guidance which will help ensure the problem, and associated issues, are resolved appropriately.

- An external consultant provides objectivity, enhances a feeling of safety, and can bring forth greater trust, allowing the process to be quicker and more successful in resolving workplace issues.

- Financially, an external consultant is more economical as this investment supports talent retention, productivity, and builds commitment.

CHAPTER FIFTEEN

WHERE ARE THEY NOW?

You may be wondering what happened to Stuart, Gary, and Josephine. As you might imagine, not all were open to the insight and wisdom I shared. Perhaps it was the resulting fallout that occurred that inspired me to write this book. At the very least, their stories allowed me to illustrate just how easy it is for things to progress when you determine that you are already awakened as a leader—even when you are still soundly asleep.

As we revisit each of these leaders, I'll describe what they did and the outcome of their situations.

STUART – AN EMPHASIS ON ROLE CLARITY

When I began working with Stuart and his team, there was a welcoming of support. The team, desperate for a change in circumstance, opened up quickly and easily.

As I learned of the dynamics involving Oliver, I saw how Stuart's management of the situation had caused it to morph into anger and frustration and why the team's negativity had been redirected onto Stuart, their leader. I met with Stuart to explain the situation, his role in it, and the options before him.

While there was pushback, eventually, Stuart listened and made changes. Oliver, unwilling to change, was terminated from the organization. The team was able to rebuild.

However, Stuart struggled to adopt a more hands-on approach with his team. The lack of support felt by the team continued to erode trust and cause anger and friction. While the team dynamics were definitively improved, Stuart was recommended for leadership coaching to further his development.

The following comments were shared by a senior member of the team as an epilogue of their team's story.

"When a person does not have the skills to be the leader, it's very difficult. Others look to their leader to take charge and to assume the direction of the team. That was an issue for our team. There was no accountability, conflict resolution, or decision-making to resolve interpersonal team dynamics.

"Now we're doing better and holding each other accountable. We're expressing ourselves more when things are not what they should be. We'll question the intent and delve a little deeper.

"Before, as a team, we would allow things to fester without calling them out. [Stuart] would maintain one-on-one meetings with members of our team. It created divisiveness. Now, we hold regular team meetings so we can all share what's going on. We're no longer siloed.

"[Stuart] is holding individuals more accountable and not allowing conflicts to go unresolved. He takes more ownership than before, and the team is more trusting of him now. He expresses himself and tells the team his feelings about a situation. There's been a real difference in his communication and his leadership ability."

GARY – A LEGACY OF LOST TRUST

Identifying what was occurring in the university department where Gary served as dean was no easy task. It took interviewing many faculty and department heads, as well as conducting a half-dozen mediation sessions before the pattern of damage and the reasons behind it became clear to me.

Once it was, I scheduled a meeting with Gary to discuss what I had learned and to provide him with advice on adjusting his leadership, confronting the damage he had created (albeit unintentionally), and reestablishing his role as the leader.

While I was delicate, the facts I laid out for Gary were indisputable. I created a timeline of situations and outcomes. I explained the damage that his well-intended policy of confidentiality, coupled with his deliberate lack of transparency, was creating. I shared strategies for curtailing the damage and rebuilding a sense of trust and safety among the faculty.

Gary didn't buy it. He remained firm in his position that he had done the right things. He reaffirmed his belief that the problems were the cause of nefarious actions by members of his faculty.

Having been hired by the head of Human Resources to address and repair the damage within this department, I shared my findings with her as well. Soon after, the university provost held a meeting with me to go over the details of what I had learned and what I recommended.

The provost removed Gary from his post. However, university politics being what they are, Gary was given another influential role—albeit one without direct reports.

In the immediate aftermath of these events, fear continued to climb, and trust among the faculty continued to devolve. The silos that were born out of this fear intensified.

The legacy of Gary's leadership left a long shadow on the department and caused irreparable damage to trust among the faculty.

I've kept in touch with a few faculty members and asked for their input in providing an epilogue to Gary's story. However, more than a decade later, even retired leaders from the department expressed their reservations about speaking with me, candidly sharing concerns of retribution should any comments be attributed to them through this book. The fear and damaged trust outlasted their careers.

The information I did receive suggested only that Gary's reputation remained poor and that he went on to lose the respect of nearly the entire faculty body. Eventually, Gary left the university to pursue another opportunity, but given the long nature of university relationships, his power remained strong in its hold on others' careers.

JOSEPHINE — A FUTURE FOR GROWTH (NOT CONFLICT)

To FIND and FIX the issues impacting Josephine, her team, and the organization, I designed a process to identify challenges, reopen communication, create planning, and rebuild collaboration.

Josephine and her team were able to gain an awareness they had lacked. While the team learned more about the interaction among their roles and the impact some were having on the work of others, Josephine became aware of her part in increasing tensions and creating conflict among her team. While these were not roles she wanted, the time they took eclipsed many of the leadership responsibilities she enjoyed.

With issues surfaced and exposed, I encouraged the team to develop a new plan without Josephine's involvement. They would determine how work would flow, who would take ownership for varying roles, and how disagreements would be resolved. One thing was clear: their plan needed to allow work to flow without Josephine's direct involvement. The team members were inspired by the opportunity.

While Josephine was caught off guard by this shift of responsibility, the team came together in a powerful way. Once they identified the path for working together, the team brought Josephine into the fold, informing her of their plan. Josephine was awestruck.

Josephine was successful in redefining her role and building trust in the team. Ultimately, by remaining supportive but not overly involved, Josephine demonstrated better conflict management.

Josephine offered the following:

"The experience (of working with Candice) was a wonderful first step. My team is now working together so well. They communicate and understand each other better. They have new tools. It's really amazing.

"This was the first step. Before, I was the glue that kept it all together. Now they don't need that. Working with Candice, the team and I have become a fully functioning group of folks. They don't need me to settle the small stuff. I've grown, they've grown, and we're now in a much better place. We're moving forward.

"I'm grateful to my company who believed in investing in our team and giving us support so that we could grow. We are a much better organization for it, and it's helped us be ready for the future."

CLOSING THOUGHTS

As you began this book, you were eager and ready to learn—to move beyond the abyss that was holding you back—to gain access to the information you need to be strong and successful and to lead your team and company to greatness.

As you read each story, I suspect you saw a bit of yourself or your former self. Perhaps you saw a colleague, a former employer, or a boss to whom you once reported. You probably noticed the lessons in this book apply to every leader and every industry. They apply to me, and they apply to you. It is at the intersection of trust, role clarity, and conflict management that leadership is determined. How you succeed in these areas will determine if your leadership will cause others to sink or soar.

As I spoke with the business owners and leaders who are quoted in this book, as well as several others whose comments didn't make their way into this manuscript, each expressed their own awakening at the concepts of how trust, role clarity, and conflict management overlap to determine what goes well and what does not.

I, too, came to greater awareness of this with each new conversation and each added chapter.

As you embark on your journey toward becoming a fully awakened leader, I hope these concepts will continue to resonate with you and guide you—that you will ask yourself often if you are doing enough to develop trust in your team while also staying involved enough to provide support and remove hurdles and barriers. That you will examine issues of accountability and ensure that responsibility and control are aligned. I expect that you will look at issues of conflict differently and stay engaged with your team in a way that allows you to nip tensions in the bud—building in their place a forum for collaborative discussion, learning, and team problem-solving.

As you practice these efforts, your team will become more self-sufficient, accountable, and capable. You will be a visionary in your leadership, having the space to think about what's next and the security of knowing you have a team in place that can follow you on that path.

QUICK FAVOR

Did you enjoy this book? Was it helpful to you? Do you hope others will read it too?

If so, may I ask a quick favor?

Please take a moment to leave an honest review of this book on Amazon. As the biggest retailer of books, Amazon influences book purchases more than anything else, so a positive review on Amazon goes a long way toward helping others find and buy this book.

I greatly appreciate your help.

ACKNOWLEDGMENTS

To Mashuri, my husband, partner, and best friend. You have been my rock and cheerleader through this journey, supporting my dream, giving me space to write, allowing me to bounce ideas off of you, and pulling me out of my own abyss when I'd be frustrated or spend too many hours writing in my office. I cannot tell you how important you have been in helping make this book a reality. I love you, and thank you so much for sharing in my commitment, as well as taking on the extra household work and family duties to make it happen.

To my daughters Madison and Avery. Your darling encouragement and patience with me while I was writing were noticed and deeply appreciated. I adore you more than words can say. I often found myself torn between writing this book and spending time with you. I can't wait to once again bake cornbread, help with art projects, watch The Goldbergs, read, relax, and cuddle with you now that this book is done.

To my friends, family, clients, and colleagues who have cheered me on, encouraged me, asked how the book was coming, and reminded me that you "can't wait to read" my book. Thank you, thank you, thank you, thank you. You have inspired me more than you know. To my Mary and Honorée, you have each helped me greatly on this path, and I am forever in your debt for guiding me on this journey.

Finally, to you, my readers. You are the muse for this book. Your success, and that of those around you, is what I want most of all.

AUTHOR'S NOTES

Thank you for reading this book. It's my first, and it has been a journey to organize and share my thoughts and ideas with you.

When I set out to write *FIND. FIX. FILL Your Leadership Gap*, I thought it would be easy. I'd share some stories; I'd offer advice; I'd provide insight and wisdom. In short, I would help people, and in so doing, I would fulfill my lifelong goal of changing the workplace. But as the work got underway, I realized just how complex this task would be.

I wrote, rewrote, and agonized. There were setbacks, including contracting COVID, moving house, and meeting an editor's deadline, all occurring in the same month. I occasionally felt lost, stuck somewhere between granular thinking and big-picture ideas. I had moments where I wanted to surrender and others where I held delusions of grandeur imagining how meaningful this book might become when it is complete. (I'm still hoping that those weren't delusions but foresight!)

Even as I struggled with this book, I knew I had more ideas to share. I am already developing a workbook as a companion piece to this book and a retreat that will allow leaders to take a deep dive into these skills while crafting their own plan for successful leadership.

I will soon begin work on the next book on this subject, focused on teams.

If you have read this, found it enlightening, helpful, educational, or even entertaining (I'm not expecting much on that last one), please send me an email and let me know. If it inspires you to work with my team or me, you can connect with us through http://www.dynamicteamsolutions.org/contact

It is truly a gift to be able to share my knowledge and ideas with you, and I hope they carry you far, helping you and the teams you manage grow and succeed.

BOOKS, ARTICLES, AND OTHER REFERENCES

Sinek, S. "Notes to Inspire" SimonSinek.com
https://simonsinek.com/notes-to-inspire/
pp. 17, 33, 114, 131, 138, 144, 154, 194, 207.

Russell, N. (2012) *The Titleless Leader: How to Get Things Done When You're Not in Charge.* Weiser.

De Smet, A., Rubenstein, K., Vierow, M. (2021, May 24) *Promoting psychological safety starts with developing leaders.* McKinsey & Company. https://www.mckinsey.com/business-functions/people-and-organizational-performance/our-insights/the-organization-blog/promoting-psychological-safety-starts-with-developing-leaders

Zenger, J. (2012, December 17). *We Wait Too Long to Train Our Leaders.* Harvard Business Review. https://hbr.org/2012/12/why-do-we-wait-so-long-to-trai

Cloke, K., Goldsmith, J. (2000) *Resolving Conflicts at Work: A Complete Guide for Everyone on the Job.* Jossey-Bass
AZ Quotes. https://www.azquotes.com/quote/1266488 (Accessed January 14, 2022)

Grant, Adam (@AdamMGrant).
"Saying "I was wrong" isn't an admission of incompetence. It's a sign that you have the humility to recognize your mistakes and the integrity to learn from them. The faster you acknowledge when you're wrong, the faster you can move toward being right." Twitter, March 03, 2021, 09:17
https://twitter.com/AdamMGrant

Brown, B. (2018, October 9) *Dare to Lead* [Audiobook]
Audible. (5:21:58-22:53)

O'Hara, Carolyn (2014, June 27). *Proven Ways to Earn Your Employee's Trust.*
Harvard Business Review.
https://hbr.org/2014/06/proven-ways-to-earn-your-employees-trust

Mraz, J. (2008). I'm Yours. On We Sing. We Dance. We Steal Things. [Audio file]. Excerpt from 'I'm Yours' by Jason Mraz used by permission. Retrieved from https://music.amazon.com/albums/B00192IOBA

Brown, B. (2018, October 9) *Dare to Lead* [Audiobook]
Audible. (0:41:26-32)

Scott, K. "3 Steps for Offering Radical Candor to Executives."
RadicalCandor.com
https://www.radicalcandor.com/3-steps-for-offering-radical-candor-to-executives/ (Accessed June 7, 2020)

Taplin, Beau. [@beautaplin] *"Lies & Silence"*
(Accessed January 2022) Instagram.
https://www.instagram.com/p/-52odpFNZ9/

Grant, A. (2021) Think Again, *The Power of Knowing What You Don't Know.*
W.H. Allen

Informative Articles about the Banking Crisis:

https://www.nytimes.com/2020/02/21/business/wells-fargo-settlement.html
https://www.ft.com/content/c6c482f8-58d4-11e3-9798-00144feabdc0

ABOUT THE AUTHOR

Candice Gottlieb-Clark is a renowned business advisor, leadership coach, conflict management specialist, and the founder of Dynamic Team Solutions. Her passion and expertise for helping businesses raise the level of their functionality, teamwork, productivity, and performance are boundless.

As a sought-after speaker and thought leader, Candice has delivered programs and keynotes to both local and national audiences, and she has been published in numerous business and professional journals, including Business Insider and Forbes.

A native of Los Angeles, California, Candice and her family now enjoy the wider expanses and outdoor activities of living in Broomfield, Colorado. In her free time, Candice enjoys cooking, hiking, snowshoeing, and taking long walks with her husband.

Connect with Candice:

www.DynamicTeamSolutions.org

LinkedIn https://www.linkedin.com/in/candicegottliebclark

Facebook https://www.facebook.com/groups/FindFixFill

Twitter @MediationGirl

Made in the USA
Middletown, DE
09 March 2022

62390894R00126